knowing

knowing

new and selected poems

by Jonathan Holden

The University of Arkansas Press
Fayetteville 2000

Cover Designer: Kai Kaneshiro
Text Designer: Ronie Sparkman

⊗ The paper used in this publication meets the minimum
requirements of the American National Standard for Permanence
of Paper for Printed Library Materials Z39.48-1984.

Library of Congress Cataloging-in-Publication Data

Holden, Jonathan.
    Knowing : new and selected poems / by Jonathan Holden.
        p. cm.
    ISBN 1-55728-551-9 (alk. paper) --
    ISBN 1-55728-552-7 (pbk. : alk. paper)
        I. Title.

PS3558.O34775 K58 2000
881'.54--dc21

                                                    99-052927

acknowledgments

The following poems have appeared or are scheduled to appear
in the following places:

The American Scholar: "The Departure of an Alphabet,"
"Righteousness"; *Black Warrior Review:* "Car Showroom"; *California
Quarterly:* "The Edge"; *Colorado North Review:* "Kansas Fair";
Crazyhorse: "Falling from Stardom"; *Georgia Review:* "Cutting
Beetle-blighted Ponderosa Pine," "Elizabeth," "The Names of the
Rapids"; *Iowa Review:* "Infrastructure," "Peter Rabbit," "River
Time"; *The Journal:* "The Wisdom Tooth"; *Kenyon Review:* "The
History of the Wedge," "Jealousy," "A Personal History of the
Curveball," "Ulysses and the Sirens"; *Many Mountains Moving:*
"Watching the Late Election Returns"; *Midwest Quarterly:*
"Liberace"; *Minnesota Review:* "Buying a Baseball," "Hotel Kitchen,"
"*The Swing,* by Honore Fragonard"; *Missouri Review:* "An American
Boyhood," "The Crash," "Landscapes"; *New Delta Review:* "Gulf:
January 17, 1991," "Western Meadowlark"; *New England Review:*
"Gould"; *Northwest Review:* "How to Have Fourth of July"; *Open
Places* and *Borestone Mountain Best Poems of 1975:* "Making Things
Grow"; *Poet Lore:* "Visiting Agnes"; *Poetry:* "Against Paradise," "The
Colors of Passion," "Losers," "One-Ring Circus," "Sex without
Love," "Some Basic Aesthetics," "The Third Party"; *Prairie
Schooner:* "Alexander Nevsky," "Ramanujan"; *Quarterly West:*
"Casino"; *Sonora Review:* "Catch with My Son"; *Southern Review:*
"Love in the Time of Cholera"; *Spoon River Poetry Review:* "Faking";
Tar River Poetry Review, "'Hollywood'"; *Virginia Quarterly Review:*
"The Secret"; *Western Humanities Review:* "Full Circle," "Oz,"
"Tumbleweed."

*I want to express particular gratitude to my editor, Brian King—for his
brilliance, his rigor, and his encouragement. He is simply the finest editor
that I have known.*

contents

from
Falling from Stardom, 1984

from
The Names of the Rapids, 1985

from
Against Paradise, 1990

from
American Gothic, 1992

from
The Sublime, 1995

contents

new poems

The Departure of an Alphabet

My father tested as a genius
in mathematics, but not
in hospitals,
where he would become
the model pupil, obedient,
passive. I was teaching
trigonometry but having trouble
deriving the formula
for the cosine of the sum
of two angles, *Alpha* plus *Beta.*
Could he help? I knew
he needed stimulation.
Mathematics was like sex for him, it
energized him. You could do it
anywhere. Even here,
I thought. But
as he hunched on the bed's edge,
his twig-thin freckled ankles
dangling from pajamas,
and began madly to cover the back
of the envelope I'd handed him
with *Alphas* and *Betas,*
I saw that he was having trouble
with his signed numbers and
his polynomial functions missed
the lines. They sagged, drooping off the edge.

After he'd died,
when I went through the attic, I found
a dusty liquor box packed high
with yellow legal pads
crowded with his algebra,

each concatenation
executed with a fountain pen
at breakneck speed
like an Olympic skier banking
through a gate, then at the margin
digging in to begin the next
concatenation, cutting
back to reach the next
parenthesis, *slant, slant;*
his mind outraced his hand;
the hand probably had trouble
keeping up;
he'd been trying
to solve Fermat's Last Theorem.
And here is how the world will end.

One day, at, say 10 A.M.
there is no more letter E.
That vowel has departed.
We try to read TH NW YORK TIMS.
Other letters are leaving. We've lost
another vowel. The letter A
has bought the farm. Cn w think?
Oops, there goes U. It's confsing.
Now O. Hw cn w cry
r ?

Sex and Mathematics

Wovan man nicht sprechan kann,
darüber muß man schweigen
              —Ludwig Wittgenstein

Making love we assume
may be defined by the equation
for the hyperbola $y = 1/x$, how
as the denominator
of a warm afternoon in May,
freighted with roses, heavy
with honeysuckle, heavy with the gravity
of one, three,
even five intervals of
unremitting time that
continues on and
on endlessly
like an ear ache
(but a good one) or
interrupted by other
intervals of simply
relenting when simply
to gulp air . . . On certain days
I swear we could see
the asymptote out there
where the curve dies.
It is a view of the sea
napping no more than
half a mile away,
royal blue and peaceful,
a flat line
while the other
becomes so steep

it hugs harder, even harder
the bed-frame,
clings to the opposite wall
like a fly, a kind
of pain, approaching
but not quite
but not
but so
close
oh
s

Watching the Late Election Returns

I remembered watching the spaceship Columbia
being raised like a public monument.
In the litany of checks
leading up to the launch,
how like the voices of little boys
the voices of the pilots had sounded,
talking with their fathers.
How determined they were to be brave,
to be unemotional.
They were scared.
They had no leeway. They couldn't
lie. One knew
that every syllable they uttered had
on pain of death
to be true.

And as I imagined the number
of trusting hands it takes
to place two humans
into the top of that pyramid—
that gargantuan toddler of a machine
slowly standing up, lifting
the glowering tread of its heel, growing
majestic as it started
like a gyroscope to lean
into the spell of its trajectory—
old sentiment welled up.
For one precarious moment—
I could hardly believe it—I thought
I was an optimist. Perhaps

I could be a citizen.
By midmorning, the subdued
voices of the soaps
had picked up
right where they'd left off,
breaking and reassembling
helplessly their treaties,
while on the other side
of the earth
Engle and Truly were helping the sun
to rise and set and rise again
and again and again and again.
I made myself a bacon,
egg, lettuce, and tomato sandwich.
I opened a beer. I began
to remember what was comfortable
and familiar: how to be cynical again.
Civic despair.

Surrender

Hell is other people.
—Jean Paul Sartre

Even now, at fifty-eight, facing
the crowded football stadium, I hesitate.
I will always hesitate. The colors
of the crowd are so many
they remind me
of foreign cooking, say paella—
a green shirt a chuck of green pepper,
white shirts tofu, (A crowd,
Auden said, "has a generalized
stink.") As I get ready
to climb up into it,
I steel myself: it's like getting
ready to subject yourself
to something that smells strong,
like sex, like vomit, like food, like shit,
like living, like dying, though
all of us used to practice
dying: There was The Fainting Trick.
We knew it couldn't be good for us,
which was why we had to do it:
sneak behind the garage,
crouch down, take ten deep breaths and
leap. *I remember this funny*
smell in my head. What am I
doing on the grass
behind the garage?
Why does it feel almost sexual,
this feeling of surrender?
It was our job to study the sensation

because we were kids—
scientists of what it feels like.
We were practicing surrender.
When I was younger, I used to drive
to Wal-Mart simply to hang out
in the presence of merchandise,
to belong. Shopping is a party
for the lonely. At night
in the suburbs the glow of Newark
makes a low blaze along the skyline.
A great party is already in session
like a war somewhere
just over the horizon.
On Saturday nights we drove toward it.
And we drove, because
by covering distance,
we accomplished something.
I'd zip the seal off
a pack of Camels, tear back
a square opening to reveal
them like a nest of cartridges,
flick my Zippo open, snick my thumb.
To inhale, exhale smoke.
To stare out, empty,
and appraise the night.
To be just another guy,
an abstract unit like an army private.
We were shoppers, consuming
northern New Jersey,
a concrete tundra of highways, roadhouses
lit up like Christmas trees, Christmas
in mid-summer in all directions,
moving lights, diesel fumes, concrete dividers.
We consumed the commodity of distance,
rate multiplied by time.

As we passed a couple,
we'd shove our collective puss out
the car window and jeer,
Go ahead fuck her. I did!
And peel out.
We feared nothing.
Felt nothing. We were anaesthetized.
Numbness of adolescence is numbness
of the lynch-mob. We were vomit
on the move. Proud of it.
Proud to be democratic, to have
surrendered ourselves,
to be dying, to be living,
to be the crowd at last
members of the species.

The Auditor

Ah, Mr. Babbitt! I appreciate
so much your willingness to take time out
from what I know must be a terrible routine
to review with us your '86 return.
Let's go back. You'd told us that you had *one*
personal checking account. That isn't true.
Our computer search reveals that you have *two!*
And in *different banks!* Your primary account
is the joint checking at First National
with your wife Carol Margaret. Is that right?
But there's this second account, at Moonlight
Savings and Loan—it's in your name alone—
that trips the computer and raises a red flag.
Now Mr. Babbitt, I don't want to be a nag,
but is your spouse aware of this account?
In "Moonlight" we find, for fiscal '86,
let's see, eighteen, no, nineteen personal checks
to a "Joan Bush." If you could specify,
in concrete terms, the job-related tasks
she does, you could help us out tremendously.
Primarily "Clerical?" "Girl Friday?"
"Consultant?" These amounts are far too small
to be "consultant fees." Something smells.

Again, please forgive my prying this way.
I can appreciate your point of view.
I've seen, from over twenty years in this
profession, how the letters "I-R-S"
can make even a decent citizen like you
a little paranoid. I might be too
(it's catching) if I were in your shoes.

But, Mr. Babbitt, your last three or four
letters to my office go too far.
"Blackmail?" Now that's a very ugly word.
Oh, we've been trained, of course. We expect
to be despised. But listen to this letter!
And I quote: *My wife says I've gone off the deep end,*
that you're probably just an ordinary guy.
I know she's right. But, they say Eichmann died
believing he was just an ordinary guy
with a nice wife and kids. He defended
himself by saying what you would say, that he
was only doing his job, right? End quote.
Mr. Babbitt, we're not out to get
you. But that letter particularly offends me.
Let's be up front. Isn't it a threat?
Now, one more letter from you like that and—
at this point I'm of more than half a mind
to have the Zenith County judge issue
a restraining order. I could sue!

And I've thought about it. The more I thought,
though, the more I realized I don't have to.
Let's get back to Schedule B. Where were we?
Male or female, most spouses, when they cheat
are rather more ingenious—and discreet—
than you have been. Forgive me, but let's suppose
some minor clerk like me had been accused
of "blackmail" by a deranged taxpayer.
I mean, in such a case, who really has the power?
The interest rate we charge on what's unpaid
is eighteen percent. Now for a month or two
that penalty's not bad. But, as you know,
the backlog is such that . . . our auditors are slow.
Take principal plus interest. What would you owe?

After four years, multiply by two.
After six years, multiply by three.
In this respect, my former client was right.
He called us "terrorists." We operate
like Chairman Mao, he said. Select a few
and make a public spectacle of you.
In full sight of the masses let them die
slowly and be left hanging out to dry.
But we don't do it; it's the interest rate;
it's nothing personal, no sir!
I mean, Lord! Just imagine if it *were*!

What if some clerk, not content to wait
and let the eighteen percent interest rate
screw you, brought up the issue of "Moonlight"
to Carol—that you had been a cheat?
Well, you've left yourself wide open, my friend,
by trying to cheat both ways. It's indiscreet
to want to have your cake and eat it too.
If fact, if memory serves me right, wasn't it you
who at parties would refer to Carol fondly
as "a kind of life collateral?"
That's what a wife should be. It makes me wonder,
though, how much a blackmailer *would* demand.
First, I think, he'd want to estimate
how strong the marriage was—the marriage bond.
The frequency and size of his demand
would have to be in direct proportion
to that and the income of the husband.
In a case like yours, these factors probably
would be determined by activity
in "Moonlight." In fiscal eighty-six
we find—let's calculate—exactly nineteen checks,
totaling two-thousand, one hundred bucks.
A current balance of a thousand bucks.

Let's see . . . Ah, yes, it's a piece of cake.

About two-fifty. And paid quarterly,
not to the IRS, mailed straight to me,
in addition to my professional fee.
Two-fifty. Like a tip, a courtesy
at least to begin with. And no checks please.

Alexander Nevsky

Music and politics are incompatible, even mutually
rejecting each other.
      —Sergei Prokofiev

All propaganda is like cartoon,
but the best transcends its use:
Riefenstahl's footage of the Nuremberg rallies
has beauty, like Eisenstein's movie
designed to give Stalin and Russia
in the figure of Alexander Nevsky
its own Beowulf.
Beauty without terror isn't beauty.
So there are intervals of dawning terror:
the Swedish army drawn in a glittering line
along a distant hillside, so far off
you can't quite tell what they are;
they're ghostly as the idea that Birnam Wood
could ever arrive at Dunsinane,
a faint tracing of an idea
like the idea of a tsunami as the line descends
toward us details begin to appear
descending in a plane from the stratosphere
we begin to see individual trees,
phylogeny resolving itself into
the ontogeny of individual furrows
in a particular field, men in armor
on horseback, hurtling forward, a clanking wave.
Clausewitz was right: Fighting is to war
what cash payment is to trade. It's naked.
They are hewing at each other, two-handed,
like day-laborers hacking at trees. *Clang*

Dunsinane! Like the pathetic tin woodsman
clanking. *Þa Byrhtnoþbraed bill of sceaþe*
brad and brunecg, and on þa byrnan sloh:
Teeth chattering, the Teutonic knights
hot on the heels of Alexander
across the lake they'd thought was frozen
find out too late their armor's weight.
It's pure slapstick—
the overfreighted Germans foundering
in the night gaps between floes as they go
under, like so many costumed children
drowning. If you're Russian, you should be
crowing—no, you should be
laughing, remembering maybe
how in World War II in the fertile
black soil district of the Ukraine
where in spring the soil is so rich
and sticky that cattle and horses could become
too deeply mired to be saved,
the German tanks bogged down, the soil
like the tricky ice, allowed the enemy in
to die.

All of us dream of wielding
like Johann Sebastian Bach
our art as a rhetoric
in the service of some large idea.
What wouldn't I give
to hold a reader as securely
as the St. Matthew Passion.
But it's a cold notion: power
and envy. The alto aria where Peter
begs God for forgiveness
for having denied Christ
in order to save his poor ass

(*I didn't know the man!*)
is frighteningly free-floating—
a squiggling of emotion that could be
attached to anything handy—
a marriage proposal, a dictator,
a pine board,
like the soprano aria in Nevsky.
After the battle when Alexander
has routed the Teutons,
a young Russian woman wanders
over the field of the dead.
She sings to the dead and the living
that whoever died a good death
for Russia, she will kiss
his dead eyes, that whoever
remains alive, she will be a faithful wife.
She will not marry a handsome man.
She wants only a brave man
who died a good death for Russia.
She is the voice of the sticky Ukraine soil,
Russia's lyric dream of itself,
Mother Russe, a humid
Venus flytrap.

After returning from Paris and America
for good, Prokofiev wrote, *We carry*
our country about with us
just enough for it to be
very powerful at first,
then increasingly so until at last
it breaks us down altogether.
You can't understand
because you don't know
my native soil.

I've got to live myself
back into the atmosphere
of my native soil, to see
real winter again,
and spring
that bursts into being
from one moment to the next.

"Prokofiev, " Eisenstein wrote,
"is profoundly nationalistic.
But not in a *kvass* and *shchi* manner
of the conventionally Russian pseudo-realists"
for whom *remesleniki* means "craftmen."
To get Prokofiev a deferment from the war
to the conservatory, Maxim Gorky wrote,
"We are not so rich that we can afford
to sole soldiers' boots with nails of gold"
before Gorky disappeared in the purges.
Wrote *Pravda* of Prokofiev's modernist dissonance,
"here we have 'leftist' confusion
instead of natural human music,"
while the Russian Association of Proletarian Musicians
says *Who? I didn't know that guy.*

I walk the bank of the Neva,
January 5, 1995. It is too cold to stroll.
Decorated with empty bottles under each bridge,
the Neva is a parade of ice floes
stopped in its tracks so suddenly the paraders staggered forward,
stumbling on top of each other
and were left this way: a frozen
mob, chaos, a frozen stumble,
the marchers caught
in absurd positions—comic?
No: Hilarious. Two men are undressing

for us tourists.
They have hacked from the ice
a map of raw water about the size of a bathtub
and will bathe in it for money, preferably
dollars. Nobody's sure any more
from minute to minute what
the ruble is worth.
A wan sun lends the waste of the Neva
a hint of glory: faint, forlorn,
already gone. The men in bathing suits
lower themselves into the gap.
They have no armor.
They are being deliberate.
There's a hint of breeze off the ice. I have to
hug myself hard. My jaws are
out of control.
I revise Clausewitz:
Lyric is to propaganda as genius is to *remesleniki,*
as blood is to polite conversation.

—for Leonard Nathan

Righteousness

is what I distrust the most
in anybody.
Even in the company of friends
my hackles go up
when they latch on
to a certain tone.

Their voices rise,
elated. They swell
with certainty.
I worry for their safety.
They're having fun, yet
this must be strenuous
as if they were doing
moral push-ups,
counting them conspicuously
out loud.

They switch to pull-ups
as if they knew
we know pull-ups
are even harder—they are
perspiring. Their eyes are flashing
with emotional honesty, with
sudden recognition as they reach
a rung still higher.

They have arrived,
their faces flushed, eyes sparkling
on this present high plateau,
a kind of unremitting
jeer, like my ex-wife explaining

why the poor need
to be fitted
with IUDs, *They have no
idea what's best for them!*

And I begin to see
what every civilization
seems to have known
all along—that
the moral impulse in us
is physical—
a necessity
to *shut somebody up
by force,*

anybody.

Infrastructure

The overnight train to Moscow is now
departing, passing
arc lights and prefabricated roofs,
the outskirts of St. Petersberg thin,
the rotting orange-slice of moon low
to the south beginning to accelerate
through the trees. We've barred
the compartment door diagonally
with a one-by-two against bandits
as the moon picks up speed, flashing now
through birches, evergreens. Frost has splayed
its claws on the window, and the snowdrifts
are racing past lickety-split, nothing
outside but a lonely seldom farm,
the hills and evergreens now bustling by
at more than a mile a minute,
the cold beginning to seep inside
as we head deeper into depression
as into the ruins of far western Kansas
where the Great Depression never
ended; the barns like elaborate clipper ships
once kept in bottles, sprawl
marooned in prairie, bleaching in the weather.
We are returning like Chekhov to the hinterland.
But there is nothing romantic about it.
What Hollywood called The Farm Crisis
is not some script with a neat
beginning, middle, and end.

In his book about the fall of the Shah of Iran, Ryszard Kapuscinski
postulates the exact moment
when a collection of angers, a collection

of hungers, a collection of people, a crowd
attains critical mass:
a moment like the moment
of inertia in physics
when something will fall,
when one policeman
walks from his post toward
one man on the edge of the crowd,
raises his voice and orders
the man to go home,
but the man doesn't run.
He just stands there looking insolently
at uniformed authority.
He glances around and sees
the same look on other faces.

When the Shah of Iran decided
to modernize his kingdom,
he thought a modern economy
like a brand new Mercedes SL
could be bought
straight off the shelf.
But when the freighters arrived
heavy with presents,
with crates of gleaming, ultra-modern
do-it-yourself toys
ready to be assembled,
the docks
were too cramped to contain
the freighters' hulls, so they had
to back up in a holding pattern,
for there were no warehouses
waiting: nothing
was ready. There was only
sand, sand and such heat

that the food which didn't spoil
and should have been trucked,
except the drivers for what
few trucks there were
had to be imported, spoiled anyway,
which didn't matter
because those with enough education,
who might have peopled the schools
to teach more people
how to assemble
the snazzy do-it-yourself machines
were not present to help,
for they'd found
you could make a far better living
elsewhere.

In St. Petersberg, we dined
under the moth-eaten velvet curtains
in the main ballroom
of the Hotel Octyabrskaya.
All along the cracked plaster walls
tufts of electrical wire sprouted
from rows of fixtures
without bulbs, without lampshades,
as if the very walls had been stricken by drought.
How like clowns the waiters looked in their tuxedoes,
solemn, stiff with dignity.
It was like having dinner with a married couple
who's in the midst of a bitter divorce
but nobody can mention it,
like the pathetic sign outside of Ogden, Kansas
proclaiming OGDEN, A CITY WITH PRIDE
which means "a city with hurt pride,"
as stricken as the Shah's fleet of trucks
gathering dust, a stage-set

left derelict in rain and sun
to bleach.

My neighbor complains about how hard it is
to find a good house-cleaner.
Others chime in: "You know it's so hard
to find good service these days."
And I think of the desperately silly
conversations in Chekhov's *The Cherry Orchard*
and of how a civilization falls.
With usura the line grows thick.
One evening, when you're dining out,
the waiters are not quite
as friendly as usual.
The next day somebody notices
a cobweb
in the southeast corner of the ceiling.
He wonders how the janitors could have missed it.
The next day it's still there.

Barbershop

ere their story die.
                —Thomas Hardy

Above us, a fan revolves,
a tireless oar
recirculating the air like orange drink
in a Woolworth's five & dime.

Outside, the downtown's slowly being boarded up,
but in Paul & Son's the mood is confident,
the conversation's slow,
about our weather and the upcoming game—
"Yep, sure looks like it could rain"—

and I believe again
in conventional wisdom.
I believe the pollsters who claim
that to understand what the American people
really think, just ask the barbers.

Paul tightens the gauze around my neck.
"The usual? Take a little off?"
"Yep." The talk drifts from the weather
to sports to politics. Everything's hedged:
"Well, I don't know about Clinton."

Above, the fan, an oar, revolves silently.
An ambulance goes by.
Paul and Son squint out their storefront at the glare:
twin sphinxes. Paul picks up his shears,
turns to me.
He resumes the harvest.

Sphinx

On every gatepost, each
distinct hawk—
its starched waistcoat puffed—
continues to keep
the census of human waste
yowling past. *One
for you. Two for blue. Three
for tree. Cow. Cow.
Cow.* Is it an oracle?
Immobile, it counts
the various types of waste product
draining the interstate.

Oh aren't they quaint! Look, Bob!
This one might be
the perfect replacement
for our jockey
holding its lantern
at the entrance
to our cul-de-sac.
It comes with an authentic
diploma certifying
its posture. Guaranteed
to stay erect
through rain, through snow, to be
your faithful butler
to barbed wire.

You ask, Are they real
or virtual? We can no longer
be certain. But it doesn't
matter. It won't complain.

Only now and then
you might hear
an orgiastic cry
It could be a hawk!
the curve of some actual
hunger. Oh, Bob,
how authentic
a memento of the time
when hunger was real,
not virtual.

"Hollywood"

"the combination of a machine and sex that Hollywood is."
—Thomas Hart Benton

It's 1937 on the sound-stage
of Twentieth Century Fox. A slatternly blonde
who resembles Faye Greener
in Nathanael West's *Day of the Locust*
but who (it's whispered) could be
Jean Harlow herself is preening
before an advancing armada of cameras.
In the wings five other identical blondes
ready to sell themselves or be sold
(I'm not sure which)
are composing their faces in mirrors.
The stage is sleazy.
It could be a burlesque show.
Or a slaughter house.

A high-school buddy of mine
boasted to me once how
he'd worked his entire hand inside
the vagina of a whore.
It was (he sniggered) like slipping
your hand into the carcass of a chicken
to fish out the packet of innards.
Why he told me this, I'm not sure.
Or why he made it sound
so ugly. It was as if, for him,
what was real, in order to be authentic
had to be ugly, like Benton
when, in his 1935 "Farewell to New York,"
he lamented "the concentrated flow

of aesthetic-minded homosexuals
into the various fields
of artistic practice.
If young gentlemen, or old ones either,
wish to wear women's underwear
it is alright with me,
but not when precious fairies
get into positions of power and judge,
buy and exhibit American pictures
on a basis of nervous whim
and under sway of those overdelicate
refinements of taste characteristic
of their kind."

Such bluster: like a tic—compulsive—
the wound a loser pugnaciously paws
as he let the *Sun* picture him,
feet planted apart, standing
his ground like a surly teenager
explaining to the camera why
he is leaving:
"The place has lost all masculinity. Even
the burlesque shows, which to my mind
are the best barometers of public taste
have lost their uproarious vulgarity."

It's such an adolescent trait—
to think that originality
and shock value
are the same.
If only *Time* hadn't in 1934
put Benton's self-portrait on its cover!
How ready he was to believe
such publicity. Now he was sure!
His brand of Regionalism was

31

the only authentic American art
possible: A realism with the guts
to show America frankly
in an unflattering light.
Like a fraternity stunt: strip her
under the glare and point,
expose for public examination all
of her pubic hair.
It was Jackson Pollack (Benton's student at
the Art Students' League) who pronounced,
"Benton had come face to face with Michelangelo . . .
and lost."

To know and yet not
be able to see what you know: Isn't that
what the blindness of Oedipus meant.
Pity and fear, saith Aristotle
(our first therapist).
That I like "Hollywood" embarrasses me
almost painfully. Benton could be
any of us
caught in the wars to make
a personal daydream
stick in the public mind, ready
to sell ourselves to be sold
and break into "pictures"—
unaware that for him the conflict
has been settled
for over fifty years.

from

design for a house

1972

Ice Hockey

Silver Lake has changed into a milky
marble floor. Wind from around the bend
drives white dust up-ice with long broom-
strokes toward the dam. The lake
talks, mutters to itself as I take
my naked fingers out into air,
grab the laces, wind them round
my ankles, winch them so tight that my feet
wilt, then work back into my gloves.
I'm done; my fingertips are stones.
I lean, then, launch out over my stick
against the wall of the wind, make the whole
map of ice begin to move, the lightning-
splits of cracks begin to move
toward me, the sleek curves of other
skaters—etched with ice-spray where
their blades bit—begin to bend like moving
rails as the network of the city thins
to a few arcs across dark wilderness
where bubbles—the unblinking eyes
of fish—come flowing by. A loose
puck wobbles over the ripples.
I interrupt it, weave it with my wand,
let the wind into my lap to make me
stall, then with a willow flick
skim it back to the distant game,
follow it, and join. The lake
begins to turn, a white wheel always
revolving, my legs robots, automatic,
kicking against the wheel
to make it spin until it streams so
fast my feet can't keep up, the wheel

35

flies out from under me, I sit down
hard on this slick seat that sears
my behind as it hisses to a halt,
then rise, chase down the game again,
thrust in my stick, grapple in the clatter.
The puck squirts free—in front of me—
alone, this rare coin, all mine.
I coddle it, nick the wheel, heave
at the wheel until it's whirling
under me in streaks, the goal swinging
into range, slap, miss, watch the puck
whiz, three guys stabbing after it
as I lean away into the force of ice
and level out, let the wind hit me
in the back, and hurl me home again
across the fleeing map.

How to Play Night Baseball

A pasture is best, freshly
mown so that by the time a grounder's
plowed through all that chewed, spit-out
grass to reach you, the ball
will be bruised with green kisses. Start
in the evening. Come
with a bad sunburn and smelling of chlorine,
water still crackling in your ears.
Play until the ball is khaki—
a movable piece of the twilight—
the girls' bare arms in the bleachers are pale,
and heat lightning jumps in the west. Play
until you can only see pop-ups
and routine grounders get lost in
the sweet grass for extra bases.

How to Have Fourth of July

Use a sledge to smash each burlapped
bale of ice into wet jewels. With
whisky-soaked mint-leaves picked
that morning, pack this ice
into tall glasses until
you can scrape the frost off
with your nail. Pour on
the bourbon, drink
till your ears ring, your teeth
ache. Drink till your lips
are numb and you smell
the summer rain in a field filled
with fresh, wild mint.

Never dunk cherry-bombs.
Under water they'll only go
boink! Light them on land
where their flash breaks the air
in half, bursts it like
a big bag leaving shorn edges
singed and smoking.

When you slaughter the watermelons,
break off such hunks that when
you bite in you get water
all up your nose.

And when it gets dark, don't go
to the fireworks. Go out into
sweet, cool thickets of
darkness, chase
the fireflies.
Clap them in jars until each jar
is inlaid with sleepy stars.

Alone

Alone is delicious.
There's no one to see.
I can eat these low clouds
and the body of wind
that's turning them into rolling
tumbleweed, eat with my hands,
get crumbs over everything,
crumbs of clouds on my nose,
in my fingernails, clouds smeared
all over my shirt and my chin.
I can lick the clouds off my fingers,
and no one can see or care if
I have as much dessert as I want.
I just reach into those blue
holes that I've left and pull out
whole fistfuls of sky, of infinity.
It's tasteless and so hard
I can chew it for hours.

Remembering My Father

As I seize the ladder by its shoulder
blades and shake it back and forth
to test its roots, its cling, test
with gummed toes each rung up
from the shadow of the north wall
into the bright desert of the roof,
the sun's weight spreads over my back,
and I see my father frowning in the sun,
his freckled back zigzagged with peeling
tan, his shoulders red, lowering a rock
into the stone swimming pool he built
by hand with boulders slithered
down on sledges from the woods,
split, rinsed off and fit—a pool
I could dive into until my ears
were so waterclogged they croaked.
I reach the top, fit
the window frame in place—the corners
mate—aim the first nail away
from the glass, sink it to its chin,
finger the next nail and prick
the wood; but as I heft the framing
hammer back to stroke, I see my father
in the cellar, frowning as he fits
his saw blade to a line, eases it back
and forth to start the cut, his breath
hissing through his nose as it always does
when he's intent. I hear my own breath
hissing through my nose. Something
silent in me starts chuckling in pure
gaiety because I'm frowning too, because
I know exactly what I look like.

Design for a House

I've placed the windows so that
the shadows that eat across
the floor and the shadow of every
lonely stone and tree in the world
all lengthen together.

With the glass I'll use,
if you concentrate you can take
the warmth out of the sunlight
in your hands like a powder and softly
brush it wherever you want, across
the face of someone you love
or blow it into their eyes.

I'm inventing a new kind of
roof. Instead of flowing over
it, the shadows of clouds come
to roost. But you can scare them
away if it gets too dark—just by
snapping your fingers—flush the whole
flock of them, make them startle and
soar away on each other's heels.

And I've a new material for walls.
After it snows, go out
into their shadow: you can wade in the sky.

Cross Bracing

Anything that had studs or
that should stand straight
wobbled. Nails peeked out.
My tables trembled when I wrote.
My counters swayed. Heavy used,
they'd wallow until they'd worked
themselves back into the pieces
that I'd cut. I couldn't understand
why houses stood, until I learned
to cross brace, to notch 2 X 4's,
snap in the brace so that the slack
studs tensed together at attention.
Now, secretly, I sometimes lean
harder than I should against the things
I've built that stand, seize them
with a suddenness to make them
shake. They won't budge. They just
give me back this secret glee
of my own full weight. I would put
cross bracing into trees, in moving
clouds and water, into my whole
life if I knew how.

leverage

An American Boyhood

There was little important
to do but chew gum, or count
the ways a flipped jackknife
caught in the dirt.
One Sunday afternoon I had an idea.
We clamped the cables of Tommy
Emory's train transformer
to a steel pie plate
filled with saltwater
and drank through our fingers
the current's purr,
dialing that bird-heartbeat
higher, riding its flutter until
both hands were bucked
out of water.
                  We knew
we were wasting our time,
though we had nothing
but time. Our parents
moved vague among their great
worries, remote
as the imperatives of weather.
And the stars appeared on schedule
to run their dim, high errands
again, leaving us lost
in the long boredom of our childhood,
flipping our knives in the dust,
waiting to find out just how
in this world we were going
to be necessary.

Visiting Agnes

By then, whatever that difficult name
was, making itself at home
in her nervous system,
had disconnected it, had all
but assumed her name, had stripped
her of her right
to communicate with her own
tongue, her right to swallow
food, her right to eat,
of the dignity to even
hold her spit, twisted
her into this small,
curiously wrought practical joke
whose eyes would squirt
this way and that, yet which
contained, still, some last seed
of Agnes, whose wheezing,
the doctor said, was laughter
at the crack I'd made about
our friend Dot's henpecking poor Pete,
part of my loud pep talk as I sat
there like some young attorney
encouraging a client, mouthing the pat
articles of law, swallowing
for the luxury of it.

Cutting Beetle-blighted Ponderosa Pine

In one week we dismantled
the little old country of the sky—
that wonderful colored
map. At anchor in its blue
harbors, between civilizations,
the big clouds would ride.
With my chain saw I opened
tracts of raw sky, cleared
until the last land in sight,
our single pier, our outpost
was one grandfather
of a tree. I chipped at
its trunk, chipped,
scaling bark-scabs off until
the hatchet skimmed wet
meat. But there were
those bluish-gray streaks
in it. I kept the saw shaking
and digging until I struck
the nerve. The tree
shivered, its spine groaning
in its throat.
When it let out a deep
croak and, shuddering,
sank into the dust, the rest
of the sky—nothing
to hold it back, sky without
a profile—rolled over
my head, more sky than anyone
can handle.

One-Ring Circus

Something of hemp there might
have been, of sawdust, pulleys,
in that swarthy woman, picaresque
in her wrestler's shoulders.
Something of tendons, of pain
in the taste of the drooling
tooth-pocked rubber bit she took
in her teeth to hang by her neck, twirling
midair, head yanked all
the way back.
When the baby elephant—tusks
hacksawed off for the tentative safety
of cash—was ushered out,
a moral might have been in the hook
at the tip of the gentleman's cane
the ringmaster like a conductor
used to collect the slack
clay folds of the animal up
onto the stool,
a moral on which even the elephant,
its eye a knot in rock,
concentrated with philosophical calm.
The April sun stained the patched sails
of the big top. Over
the din of the generator
an electric organ maintained the fanfare.
You might have smelt elegy there—
the idea of a brass band, tubas
harrumphing, spitting the sunlight, nodding
yes up Main Street on Saturday morning,
new paint on the wagons,
their fool's-gold gingerbread cornices

polished, the horses' sides
flush with the June sheen of meadows,
the lions dragging the rasps in their throats—
a parade as startling, brave
as the tulips. None of this
could happen.
Though the clown in the baggy pants
was too drunk to be sad,
and the juggler could never quite find
all the red balls at once,
this was not even the Circus of Failures.
It was no more than the world, no more
than the sum of its parts.

Peter Rabbit

The sunlight was dull, it might have been
morning or evening before the word *Don't*
was said. The grass, if there were grass, might
have been gray, it didn't make any difference.
The temperature of the air outside the burrow
was normal. *Don't.* It cast all the shadows.
The sun shrank back into focus. He could see.
Under that harsh brilliant judgment
each whetted blade of grass had a black shadow.
And a gate was rearing against the sky,
a rebuke, a giant affront. He squeezed under it,
his heart twittering. *Scritch. Scratch.*
He could hear—a rake, a bee fizz as it rose
from a daisy, the wind's restless crowds
in the high reaches of the oak trees behind him,
wind encompassing fields for miles, birds
swinging on it, sparrow trapezes, wind,
enough sound to cover his tracks, *don't,*
don't, to make sly twitches, faint substitutions
of grass that could be other stealthy creatures,
decoys to draw the fire of Mr. McGregor,
as Peter, now sick with hunger, crept
toward the clenched hearts of the lettuce,
thinking, don't touch the hidden parts you've
heard about, don't finger the wet leaves, don't
spit them out. "Stop! Thief!" It sharpened
the shadows. *Don't. Don't.* The leaves poised.
Each wisp of darkness held out the cool
palm of its hand, its hollow of safety, a silk
suit to slip into, try on, cast off. He'd never
noticed such terrain. How its curves console,
its hills reveal. Without Mr. McGregor,

he might never have seen a pot before. "Stop! Thief!" The light was a nuisance. Each row was a bootstep. A scramble. A heartbeat. Each second a question. Each door a new answer. The gate was a daydream, and he was alive.

Why We Bombed Haiphong

When I bought bubble gum
to get new baseball cards,
the B-52 was everywhere you looked.
In my high school yearbook
the B-52 was voted "Most Popular"
and "Most Likely to Succeed."

The B-52 would give you the finger
from hot cars. It laid rubber,
it spit, it went around in gangs,
it got its finger wet and sneered
about it. It beat the shit
out of fairies.

I remember it used to chase
Derek Remsen around at recess
every day. Caught, he'd scream
like a girl. Then the rest
of us pitched in and hit.

Births

My parents must have kept the cat
for us—our education, a live
experiment. *Chippy,* true to her name,
would regularly retire
to the wicker laundry basket
we'd lug up from the cellar,
where, on stained baby blankets,
while we all closed in to watch,
her body would obey its orders, produce
more glistening raw life
while we encouraged her, stroking,
Nice Chippy, longing to communicate
yet shy because in each emergency
the cat knew more than we
did or ever wanted to. She seemed to be
listening, and as one came
would speak—not a *meow* but a word,
we were sure, meant something.
Then, with her solicitous tongue,
she'd complete the kitten.

I remember, myself, in the shiny,
tile delivery room, unable
to help my wife—
the clarity of her loneliness.
There's privacy in pain.
The degradation is too intimate:
it must remain a secret.
And that company we press on the suffering
isn't for them. Even mother,
who regrets that in the roar
of nitrous oxide she forgets

our births, who'd explain to us
that perhaps Chippy was afraid—
that a cat can't understand
what's happening to it—could remind us
in her next breath that all except one
kitten must be "put to sleep"
with chloroform—a word which,
I was certain, meant a sweet drifting
off to dream as my parents
tucked the kittens in, kissed them
goodnight.

For a week, Chippy would prowl
the house, a walking minuend, meowing,
then, as mother predicted, would forget.
I wondered where they went until
among some wood scraps in a cellar
corner I lifted the lid of a rusty pot
to stare at three of them in bed,
clumped cold, their puny countenances
squinched shut. The sweet
faraway hint of chloroform
I soon forgot
until one afternoon, my parents gone,
with a kitchen chair I reached
the bottle. Strange as sex, it was
stronger than a smell: it was a force
that made my heart reverberate,
arranging, grimly tightening
the room, taking
charge of my breath, more serious
than anything I'd meant, worse
than an experiment.

Catch with My Son

It's evening
out on the slovenly lawn
as he tries to connect us
with a straight line.
But the loose thing
has no sense of direction.
It gets snarled in the grass.
I hold it up again
in the soft remnants of sun
for him to see
and pull it taut,
take aim, hint
what I could do with it.
Draw a bead on the walnut tree.
Blow his head off cleanly.
I wind up again
slowly
like stroking a knife
on a whetstone, *silk,*
silk, till the edge
of the edge is out of sight
and the skin on the thumb
drawn against it
shudders. I wind up
again, then roll
it to him.
He balances it
like a spear
between us carefully
aligning the air.
He's laughing.
A line sings

through my head. A line
goes through my hand.
Giggling,
he winds up again
but does not throw.
The line will go anywhere
he wants, this
is better than throwing.

To a Boyhood Friend: How We Changed

I know now where
it starts. In Ortman's
garage, with the ancient
smell of gasoline, you
on your back, pinned
down by your buggy,
your hands out of sight
reading Braille patiently,
unbolting something
I can't see.
I am standing next
to the jack, in the bad
light, as in the entrance
to a mine, the only
person there who is not
working. Somewhere
a grease gun sneezes.
One after another, cars
phone in, sending Roscoe
out the door to crank
the pump and make it
sing like water
running.

I stand there, useless,
my hands still clean,
trying to piece together
from your grunts
how long it will be
before the buggy's ready
to drive back to that rink

we wore in Remsens' field.
I am not thinking
about machines. I am
imagining how the wind
will blabber at our teeth
as we chain-saw dirt
around one end, burst
back into the loud
blue haze we'll leave
over the buzzing
straightaway before
we come sliding into
home again, spewing
the dirt and be
off, making the woods
jittery downhill.

Jimmy, twenty years
it's taken me to say this.
Hanging out in Ortman's
was so dull it was like
pain. I remember almost
nothing. What I picked
up about machines was
this: how shy the thin
muscle of the light
might be along
the silvery forearm
of a wrench,
the delicate hinge
in the wrists of ratchets,
their exact tick,
how Roscoe's swollen hands
could get the leverage
to wedge around and

loosen blocks I could
no more budge than
two hundred pounds
of frozen sod,
the cold chaste way
the sun might touch
the edges of the clouds
outside. The rest
was useless.

Making Things Grow

All day we've had to haul around
and readjust the garden hose's coils
to keep the mouths in that thin soil
kissed evenly. They must be loose
unpuckered. I want them ready
to receive the sun, and wildly,
the way our daughter wrings milk out
when she makes her bottle chirp
or drinks up sleep, her paws curled
as if clutching out at it, the way
she digests the yawn that widens
through her arms each time she hoists
herself upright with her hands, or laps
up what it is she studies in my eyes.
That's what the garden, though it won't
wake me up at night, expects of me,
what all unkissed places everywhere
expect, the tongue expects, what this
lonely place on the neck expects and
what, on tiptoe, this place on the
throat expects. And this place
here. And here.

from

falling from
stardom

1984

Liberace

It took generations to mature
this figure. Every day it
had to be caught sneaking off
to its piano lesson and beaten up.
Every day it came back
for more. It would have been
trampled underground, but
like a drop of mercury, it was
too slippery. Stamped on,
it would divide, squirt away
and gather somewhere else, it was
insoluble, it had nowhere to go.
All it could do was gather again,
a puddle in the desert, festering
until the water had gone punk, it
was no good for anything anymore.
It wears rubies on its fingers now.
Between its dimples, its leer is
fixed. Its cheeks are
chocked, its eyes twinkle. It
knows. Thank you, it breathes
with ointment in its voice,
Thank you very much.

The Secret

At first the secret seems a form
of wit, a concealed weapon.
And for the man working underground
when he comes home from his job,
it can set the unimpeachable
odor of cut onions into poignant relief,
the cat sunning itself in the corner,
all the lost and beautiful laziness
of the domestic.
At first it's as light
as a word or a whisper of spice or a name.
It's the vocabulary of a new
tongue the body memorizes as it goes along,
a tongue it recites to itself to stay whole
until the secret refuses
to be a word anymore.
It will not be abstract.
It gathers things to itself, collects mornings,
days, it is gaining shares of the night.
It takes on weight.
Wherever you walk, you haul it
behind you, room after tall invisible
room, and wherever it drags,
it picks up more of the world
until it must surely be conspicuous
as if a man limping home dragged with him
the last city he came from,
where part of him still lives
like the dark face of a woman who goes wet
to his touch, the keyboard
he snaps shut in his briefcase
when he thinks he is done,

the secret so well fed, so extensive
now it is truly too much
for one to carry;
yet neither the secret nor the small
pale hours he has left outside it
will ever hear of the other
unless he lets them.
They can only deny each other—
the secret that puts on his clothes
in the morning, that carries
his briefcase, that goes through
the distant gestures of his occupation,
the denial that, so long
as he can bear it, is
him, the secret he can no longer
keep.

Losers

The best part of NFL playoff games
is those shots of the losing bench.
                    —overheard in a bar

Without their helmets
their faces betray everything:
defeat, an open political
scandal. Some are
crying. I want to thank
them. They admit. I'd like to shake
their homely, trustworthy hands.
But they just sit there,
each of them going
over his own private score
again, checking the bland words
of his rejection

like a man sorting slowly
through all of the flattering
hackneyed constructions
his lover had once placed
on his eyes, on his mere
hands—*I'll do anything*
for you—each word a smooth
flat stone, a *tabula*
rasa he still strokes absently
under his thumb, remembering
when the act of simply
unbuckling his belt
was cruel,
a command that could crush
her parts of speech to a single

vowel, the same
stark question begging
his answer—a short
hard retort he'd thought only he
could give again
and again—what he'd always
suspected of his true
worth, the secret he'd scarcely dared
whisper even to her—

Not like these
men, slumped on the losing
bench, staring ahead, trying
to comprehend the rudiments
of some old standard system of
weights and measures
they'd once learned they had
to go by—
these men who, out of
power now, relieved
of their secrets, are as honestly
miserable as they look.

The Edge

High up on the bike, my son
Zack talks a blue streak
as I stride with him,
aiming him, sighting his fat
front tire wavering
along the sidewalk. We stride
through a narrow country
of sunshine, step off
into shadow, ford a bright creek
and flash through a place
of islands and sunponds.
We both see everything
this morning, husk of a firecracker,
wisp of cotton, rusty edges
of light on the grass blades
as if we both knew
we would never see this country
again: we are leaving
today, moving west,
and the history of each wet
lawn is suddenly clear. We are
moving. I am trembling
with him. The bike
tips. He oo's as I catch him, scared
just enough, half rapture,
half fear as he teeters, balancing
in both countries at once,
right on the edge and
knowing it, knowing this
is important, that the next
moment he could find out
how quaint the Old World is,

be looking down, see
where its shores curl on the map
as the weight of him soars
out of my arms
for the last time,
and only I will be left
trembling as on the night
he was born, when,
home again, alone, I babbled
as he is now, I was singing,
laughing out loud with no one to hear,
watching a cloud drift like a dune
that I knew would never
repeat itself, over a waning
three-quarter moon,
thinking, *This is the last
time this will ever
happen, thinking only
god, that cloud, this night,
that moon!*

Elizabeth

The orphanage in Seoul
might as well have been
in another galaxy,
our photograph of her
a star, the black and white
suggestion of a face,
light shaped to a cheek,
formed in tiny hands,
the darkness of deep space.

For months that winter, we
observed her through this smudged
aperture, our own star
Elizabeth,
until we believed enough
to set up the second-hand crib
in the warmest corner.
We were enlarging her
when we got a letter.

More than a lifetime it takes
when a star goes dead
for the darkness to arrive.
We stared at what we held
in our hands—shadow and light,
a photograph of nothing—
and knew in our half-formed grief
that we were holding nothing
we hadn't held before,

nothing more than the faint
glow where a star has been,

this feeble wavering light
that still fitfully reaches
us across light years
as if from somewhere
             nothing
as real as any star.

Falling from Stardom

—for A.

When only the human remains,
our two human faces licked clean
of disguises like two friends,
I understand what an ex-lover meant
when she said she was tired
of fucking celebrities,
how this star director
who confessed he'd grown bored
with practicing stunts
on one trapeze at a time
turned out to be
no more than his assortment of methods.
The persuasion in his hands,
even the tropical weather moving
through his melancholy eyes
seemed to her ulterior.
On the mattress with him
she was a mirror.

I have friends who are afraid
to say something trite.
Every rejoinder must top what was just said.
Their gossip's hilarious;
it's a compost of envies. They'll tell you
the sex habits of each president.
At 50, they would still live as we did
before we gave up counting
the nervous thrills in this world
and bore our children.

But their mouths are chameleon, their faces
want definition, are composites of all
our faces, and we
are the score which they cannot stop keeping.
When they lend us themselves
they use the word *love.*
They would finish with us
as with a piece of heavy equipment.
Their motion's a form of immunity.
Loneliness gives them freedom to move.

I wake with you now, and for the first time
that I can remember,
I envy nothing.
The morning's singular;
it will not refer.
Am I naive?
Is this some child's drawing?
There's a blue brook. On it, a boat.
One cloud. One bird. The sun
faithful, always right-handed,
scatters its sticks of lemony candy.
Everything's loyal.
The boat wants only to be a boat,
the cloud a cloud,
the bird bird,
the brook.
If the word *love* means anything
it must be like this—
how two sticks of sun that fall in the brook
can shine all morning, shine
beneath fame, the water descending
without demur, filling
one place at the time.

from

the names
of the rapids

1985

The Names of the Rapids

Snaggle-Tooth, Maytag, Taylor Falls—
long before we measured with our eyes
the true size of each monstrosity,
its name, downriver, was famous to us.
It lay in wait, something to be slain
while our raft, errant, eddied
among glancing pinpricks of sun
and every bend giving way to bend
seemed a last reprieve.
But common terror has a raw taste.
It's all banality, as when
you stare straight into a bad cut—
this sense of being slightly more
awake than you might like.
When the raft pitches sideways off
a ledge, what you land on is less
than its name. It's a mechanism. None
of the demented expressions
that the fleshly water forms
over that stone profile
is more than another collision,
a fleeting logic lost and
forming, now lost in the melee.
When the world is most serious,
we approach it with wholly open eyes
even as we start the plunge
and the stone explanation.

The History of the Wedge

In the brisk, pleasant voice of a surgeon
introducing his choice operation
the Air Force assured us how strictly
professional it is. *Armament,*
radius, objective: each word neutral
as a steel tool rinsed and drawn clean
from the Latin—a scalpel, a sterilized needle.
And we watched the latest knife:
five General Dynamics F-15s
like a five-card hand on the prowl
curve out over downtown Topeka and cut,
break east with a spurt, a sharp
black smudge, and they're off on a new
vector, they are carving together;
that whole hand is rolling over
like one moving card revolving itself
to flash all five spades at once,
chased by the ragged mass of their roar,
the heavy furniture they trundle behind them
being hauled, torn over every rough floor
in the sky, rolling over roofs, ripping
and mending as the sixth svelte blade
clicks into formation, completing
this steadily traveling phalanx,
and there in the hazy autumn sky
we see this oldest formation of power,
abstract force focused in one ghostly
capital letter: Δ. The idea cruises
above us this afternoon, meeting
no resistance at all, circling
as if looking for victims. Nothing up there
to rape, but it can't stop moving;

it's coming back low, flat over the field
to shock it for kicks, the whole
history of the wedge is bursting
straight up the sky, trailing white crepe-
paper streamers in one, grand, Fourth-of-July
finale, fanfare proclaiming its victory,
Force flaunting itself, flexing
its engines, crowing, deafening us
with its form of laughter
as it lets its whole tool hang out
unsheathed, vertically, over 10,000 feet,
shaking it, shoving it in our faces.

Car Showroom

Day after day, along with his placid
automobiles, that well-groomed
sallow young man had been waiting for
me, as in the cheerful, unchanging
weather of a billboard—pacing
the tiles, patting his tie, knotting, un-
knotting the façade of his smile
while staring out the window.
He was so bad at the job
he reminded me of myself
the summer I failed
at selling *Time* and *Life* in New Jersey.
Even though I was a boy,
I could feel someone else's voice
crawl out of my mouth,
spoiling every word,
like this cowed, polite kid in his tie
and badge that said *Greg*,
saying *Ma'am* to my wife, calling
me *Sir*, retailing the air with such piety
I had to find anything out the window.
Maybe the rain. It was gray
and as honestly wet as ever. Something
we both could believe.

Buying a Baseball

As I turned over in my palm
that glossy little planet
I was going to hand my son,
I was wondering how
it could still cost the same
as when I was his age.
Around came the brand:
Rawlings. Made in Haiti.
Like those poor city kids
I'd heard have no idea
that milk came from a cow,
I'd never known before
where baseballs came from.
They were always there
in the stores in bins, stitched
tight as uncracked books,
each with its tiny trademark,
Made in Hell.
We'd test the tough seams
along both fingers' links
to get a thrill of power
remembering how to fake
a staggering grounder out
so it would leap to the mitt
at our convenience,
how that black magic squeezed
in the core would make it
spark off the bat
with a high, nasty *crack*
you could mistake for no
other sound in the world.

The Swing, *by Honore Fragonard*

*From this painting alone . . . one could have
predicted the entire French Revolution.*
          —Gerhardt Weis

Her pink chubby fingers trusting
the rope, one slipper flying
off one toy foot, a toy

herself, a girl is sailing through
the silly leaves. She hasn't heard
of the guillotine. She is plummeting,

rising, into and out
of the pitfalls of pleasure,
her petticoats like a parasol blooming

over her Baron de Saint Julien
fainting in the bushes with desire
as she leaves him again to go high

into a leafy canopy that seems
to be connected to nothing—
How can it hang on any longer?

But she isn't thinking:
she's breathless, in a flutter,
a swoon as when, shopping, the mind

stops—We think, *This can be mine*—
and we give ourselves away just
as easily as this ignorant girl

secure on her plump velvet cushion
starting back down through the silly leaves
while the rope groans and holds,

now owning, now thoroughly
owned by the rush of the foliage,
by gravity.

River Time

Day after day we fell deeper
in love with gravity. Mornings
we could hardly wait to catch up
with the water. In tandem, making
aluminum shout over gravel, shush
up in the sand, I and my taciturn
friend from Minnesota would drive
our canoe down the bank at the river,
steady the boat for Tom's small son,
scramble in ourselves and then surrender.
"River time" we called it for a couple
of days, until we forgot the old time,
river time became absolute time,
the current our clock. We had struck
some common, rock-bottom pace.
We were drifting in step
with each floating leaf, with every
unblinking blister of foam
under the channel's silent spell,
no need to paddle
except to adjust to the ticking
current, trowel a slow whirlpool, a furl
filling up in the ripples we trailed,
correcting our timing to keep
in perfect stride with the law.

A dozen canoes, one canoe to a bend,
moving with the caravans of moving fog.
By noon everyone would be stoned
on pot and the hundreds of pounds
of beer we had brought.

The architect and his wife, all
the assistant professors, the various
students, even my friend in the stern
would be rendered inert,
complacent, unwilling to speak.
Whatever it was we might need
we would let the river decide.
We'd unbuttoned ourselves from our words;
we'd jettisoned the ballast
of the usual week, left all that
upstream on the bank. It made us
pleased with ourselves, day
after day, simply to register
the faithful way those banks continued
unfolding themselves and tree followed tree
through the warm, intermittent rain.
The rain meddled in everything.
It riveted the tarnished water, shooting
plump bolts through and through it,
spot-welding reflections of the sky.
The rain hopped all over your tarp
and in the hot swarm of your hair.
It was on your tongue, in your joints,
in the steam of your breath,
until you forgot to shoo off
the drops that alit, forgot
the wet yoke sticking tight to your back,
the hot swamps you lugged around
in both boots, forgot even the mush
squeezing foam between your toes.

Long before our last night on the river
we were wet beyond hope,
we could get no wetter. That night

someone's flashlight beam nicked
a flat rock with a necklace
curled on it—soft, precious—
a copperhead blocking the path.
In a hutch of clear plastic
anchored by rocks, we skinned
and steamed together. Outside, a bonfire
shooting twice as high as a man
gave its fierce heat to an armload of
stones, coaxing them into embers.
We took turns steering to the tent
between tongs each red-hot rock
and scattered water on it,
making steam snarl, blinding
ourselves with blast upon blast.
Naked, whooping, we'd charge
at the river, then crawl back
in the blur of that stifling incubator
where we were babies again,
the language was skin,
you could forget even your name.
Of the girl who stole with me later
back to my tent, I remember only
that she was wet wherever I parted her,
alluvial, how the graceful curved way
her hair fell seemed like a word
I had learned once—anonymous,
familiar. She was all words at once.
And I remember how, halfway
toward dawn, the cries of two
whippoorwills kept opening
and closing like twin arteries
while we answered each other.

Next morning, our last, the river
was iron, frying, leaping
in the light rain as people numbly
traded partners. I carried
my pack to the girl's canoe,
and we took the current's smooth
old hand, let it take our hand,
and the drizzle lifted, the complexion
of the water cleared,
and we could see in the interior
the dark, slow slippage of bass.
Oars shipped, we watched a moccasin
give us the slip, scribble away
deep in that gray-green psalm.
And far out through the brush
and the mist's restlessness,
a bobwhite swiped its whetstone.
We just let the boat drift,
pleased with the lull of inertia,
foreseeing no end, ready
for only what could be more water,
knowing that around the coming bend,
across another misty clearing,
the profile of the trees would be
unbroken, curving into the next
bend where another old tree
would be succumbing, tempted
to drink, its crooked reach
combed by the water, waking
the current under the cut-bank
before the water would widen,
and we'd stall
in an even purer silence,
dim canyons of boulders, of twilight
deep in the green requiem below

easing silently under our bow,
the river adagio.

That afternoon, reluctant, we beheld
through gray, scarcely seeping air
stumps of a broken bridge
and down both banks a dump,
a great population of junked cars—
bodies which, once pushed, went churning
headfirst and, catching
on roots, had flipped on their backs
with the rest of the rusty scree—
a scorched city lost under the trees—
until the next bend gathered us
in, a crowd of people came slowly
around, walking on the rocks
where two trucks were parked
and a road—a shock of sky in the trees—
petered into the floodplain stones
and at the shallows stopped.
And two men, two fat retarded twins
in bib-overalls, two comical men,
humpty-dumpties with rotted mouths,
were circling my Minnesota friend,
spitting words, gesticulating at him,
arguing he better move his goddamn
hippy van because this floodplain
here belonged to *them,* while Tom,
from the cab, glared down with a stiff
slightly puzzled stare, white-knuckled
in the face. And the look the architect
slipped me meant something dirty
he knew about: it meant *Move off.*
We walked our canoe across the ford,
shoved it up on mud. The rain

returned, through the rain
we watched one brother squat
behind Tom's camper to jot the plate;
Tom's truck wallowed, bucking
like a dog digging, spewing back rocks.
But the fat guy expected it. He lurched
the gap to his pick-up's cab,
and the long .22 automatic he pulled
discharged its six dried-twig snaps
at the back where Tom's boy bounced
as the rear of the fleeing camper
leapt over the crest and out of sight.

In fistfights the hate-scent can be so strong
it gets the tightening circle half-incensed.
But anger, in a shot, goes so abstract
at first you can't even recognize it.
Just this detached small-kindling spark.
Could it be some practical joke
over which both brothers on the opposite bank
now chortled and whooped like Laurel and Hardy:
they were slapping their knees, congratulating
each other with whops on the back? *What time
was it?* All I knew was how wet and cold
and pathetic we looked, searching
for footholds in the mud, slipping,
digging in our heels again and heaving
our canoes up the bank—
how sick of this desolate river and the rain.
At last the road like a room in the woods.
Token of a hug was brusque enough good-bye
to the girl, who wanted to get away
as much as I did. And I talked
with the architect of what we'd seen,
our words—the words we needed—seeping

slowly back into our extremities.
Then the small chagrin of comfort—
dry socks like Christmas presents,
the reassuring idle of a car—
our words now flooding back luxuriously,
words for that godforsaken place
and how to get out of it.
Later, with time enough to bathe,
the words for our excuses, the redundancies,
the first, sweet, foreshadowing
of shame.

Lust

You would have had to measure
that fair countenance of hers a hundred
times before you would suspect:
Susan was, when this was happening,
so beautiful. The finest murmur,
the slightest rumor passing in her face
you would have sworn implied a pure
intelligence, sworn that when
she looked amused at what you said
it was because her calm eyes
had read between the lines.
Only over time would you have seen
what I, too late, began to notice,
that she was always amused, her smile
was not authentic: there was
something covert about it;
it was askew, a thin moon
that stayed up far too long.
It was almost a smirk, a politeness
that mocked being polite
like her words, always a little too
sweet. Her answers, when, too late, I learned
to hear, would give you your own words
back, yet with the wrong taste.
But I was young and dumb;
her blond hair was proverbial,
and the body has its own rhetoric—
she was proof of that cruel joke.
So on this cold, windless afternoon
in the mountains when I hiked
over the Douglas firs' blue shadows
up the County Road to the mailboxes

by her house, knowing it was not
to fetch the mail, and opened
the side door at her muffled *Come in,*
I checked my watch and,
dumb as a man, calculated
how long the house would be secure—
this snug, strict little house so nicely
dusted and picked up, the winter
sunlight lost in the corners, discarded—
two hours until, upstairs, Leslie
would wake up.

The body, when it doesn't have
to explain itself can be so
eloquent. An act of perfect
timing alone—a fake, a linked series
of strides to the hoop, the dunk—
looks exactly like intellect.
The move was *brilliant,* we say,
as if it were something we
had thought. Or think
of the beautiful stations of lust
linked one after the other.
They form the perfect replica
of love—love, which is intelligent.
No matter how shrewdly each body
uses the other, you would swear
that both partners were true,
that they could trust each other.
You would swear, I think, to almost
anything, forgetting
the way an athlete hurt
on the field might be mistaken
for being, at that moment, sincere,
that the aftermath could be

as randomly littered with wreckage
as Susan's living room was
two Aprils later when, hailed
from the mailbox to be offered hashish
I looked the place over.
The divorce was soon to come through.
Plump Leslie sat dazed in a corner
while Susan and people I didn't
know, like a ring of campers
on the rug, warmed themselves
around the ashtray.
The house smelled all wrong,
but I lingered there simply to look
at Susan, imagining the earnest
almost clumsy way she had loved
to make our teeth bump, had licked
my back as that pink bath
slowly, all afternoon, sank
from lukewarm to cool around us.
I lingered just to look at her.
To look.

Some events, when held to the light,
you could pull like a sock inside
out. The day I accepted in a faint rain
Susan's ride up the mountain
in her old Dodge wagon with the shimmy,
Leslie, cherubic, her white German hair
cut in bangs, sitting in the back
with two other children,
it was simply to look at Susan
who, her stale smile a wisp of a moon,
with a ghastly pleasantry took every curve
up the canyon too fast.
She is insane. It was as if

I had owned the evidence all along
but hadn't known the right word,
that word which maybe always arrives
oblique like the oncoming
car which now did, as Susan,
stuck in her smile, not
slowing, spun the wheel
as if to turn into our side road,
and we came to rest, a stalled
windmill, intact in the other lane.
Then she turned the key and,
ignoring the children's slight
confusion, started the pull
up the wet dirt road, asking me
finally, as if somehow baffled, why
I seemed so nervous.
Do you know . . . how lucky . . .
I bumbled an answer, it was too
obvious. She just smirked to herself.
And when, on foot at last, I was
set free in the gray silence,
I must have been halfway down
the twin ruts to my cabin
when it struck me: she had tried
to kill us. I looked back then.
Her car still hadn't moved.
It idled in the mist where she watched,
her want making me able to want,
want, even as I turned away.

Casino

Under this oppressive, slippery sky
of mirrors, where the promise of cash
is a fragrance, voluptuous,
you could forget the ways of the gods.
One pull on a handle, *bells! lights!* the world
could go all to pieces, be turning
itself inside out as if in love
with you. A slot machine spits
me a coin. I'm unmoved by gifts.
Luck, you can see, was never anything
less obvious than a lady slipping
her slightly fat shoulders from her robe
as she picks some victim out
to throw herself at.
And winning, though it's the perversion
hardest to resist,
may be more dangerous than losing.
A man thirty years married once told me
how most of one wonderfully mild,
wronged Tuesday morning, after drying
the breakfast dishes, he lounged upstairs
in his marital bed,
committing deliberate adultery
with a family friend,
how the pale light of her body,
filling the room, contradicted
the worn shag rug, the famous old crack
in the bedroom ceiling.
The perversity of it awed him—
his shockingly clear sense of detail,
that this beautiful head, eyes half
closed, her hair slicked hard

around her temples,
could replace his wife's bruised face,
as we'd say, *in the flesh,* could be this
literal. He could no more stop
than could any of these broken people
release the handles that keep pulling
them, though they know as well as we do
that the next jackpot will drive them crazy,
how luck and adultery
are only two of the many low religions,
each waving its claim to make a word flesh,
and the gods remain abstract
as money, as love, as they ever were.

Kansas Fair

*There can be no "normal life" until every oppressor swine has
ransomed with his blood the blood of this brave lad.*
        —from an IRA funeral eulogy

Sorefooted, sunburnt, I escape
the hot pelt of the crowd for a little
shade, to watch from the sidelines
people trading places. A baby,
eyes bugging, bobs by in its knapsack.
An old couple, in pursuit
of something severe and private,
hesitate, then find their narrow
seam through the traffic.
And as I sit there, pulled
by the argument of every smell—
cigar smoke, french fries, suntan oil—
by the whole, complex, bittersweet
scent of the gathered human—I wonder
what it would take to convert
these farm hands with mustard streaks
on their beards, so they might believe
in history. A scuffle? An explosion?
The helicopter, a dark locust swarm
spinning down over the trees?
I do not believe in one history,
but that among us the believers
are the dangerous ones.
Their minds are elsewhere.
When they eye a crowd from the side,
they are counting the bodies.

And that it's lucky to be in the shade,
to be so prodigally bored,
resting one's feet, certain that
all this afternoon and the next, nothing
important will happen.

Ramanujan

It was Mr. Littlewood (I believe) who remarked that "every positive integer was one of his personal friends."
    —G. H. Hardy

This modest, mousy little boy from India
could reel off pi's digits to any
decimal place his classmates dared him to.
No mean feat. But for Ramanujan it
was a breeze. Pi was merely one of his
first cousins, in fact, a favorite.
And his cousins were innumerable.
Each day when school let out, he'd retire
to the silent playground where they waited,
a windless plot with neither sun nor moon.
A silent playground—it was a funny place,
part civilized and partly wilderness.
It had some cultivated sections, but
all the rows, like footprints in the snow,
simply petered out into a white
fastness that was neither far nor near.
There was no definite horizon there.

Without a word, Ramanujan would sit
down among his friends and question them.
Some were persnickety at first, but if
he scattered seed and sat still long
enough, they'd hop right up to him.
Like sparrows, they'd eat out of his hand.
And once a number had confessed, Ramanujan
was its intimate. Each face touched off
for him its sly Gestalt: it pulled the trigger
that the kindly puss of your old car pulls

as you pick it out among the traffic,
idling with its crotchety click-click;
it was the smell of home cooking.
When Hardy once casually remarked
that the integer 1729
on a taxi seemed "quite dull," Ramanujan
quickened. Why no, it was the smallest sum
of two cubes expressible in just two ways.

When he died, his room was packed. The wall,
the clock, the close air bristled with his friends.
As he expired, softly they slipped off;
those countless cousins, all without a word,
without jostling a single speck of dust,
without leaving the slightest trace behind,
without touching anything, fled back
to haunt that playground where for thirty years
he'd shuffled out and sat. The rest of us,
still stuck here in the shambles, go right on
sneezing with the seasons and galumph around
grabbing the daffodils too hard, bruising
the fruit, ordering the weeds to state their names,
waiting for the scent after the thunderstorm,
the shot, the drenching accident, to be
the Ramanujans of experience.

from

against paradise

1990

A Personal History of the Curveball

It came to us like sex.
Years before we ever faced the thing,
we'd heard about the curve
and studied it. Aerial photos
snapped by night in *Life,* mapping
Ewell "The Whip" Blackwell's sidearm hook,
made it look a fake: the dotted line
hardly swerved at all.
Such power had to be a gift
or else some trick; we didn't care which.
My hope was on technique.
In one mail-order course in hypnotism
that I took from the back-cover
of a comic book, the hypnotist
like a ringmaster wore a suit,
sporting a black, Errol Flynn mustache
as he loomed, stern but benign
over a maiden.
Her eyes half-closed, she gazed
upward at his eyes, ready
to obey, as the zigzag strokes
of his hypnotic power, emanating
from his fingertips and eyes,
passed into her stilled, receptive face.
She could feel
the tingling force-field of his powers.
After school, not knowing
what to look for, only
that we'd know it when it came—
that it would be strange—
we'd practice curves, trying
through trial and error to pick up by luck

whatever secret knack a curveball took,
sighting down the trajectory
of each pitch we caught
for signs of magic.
Those throws spun in like drills
and just as straight,
every one the same.
In Ebbets Field I'd watch
Sal "The Barber" Maglie train
his batter with a hard one at the head
for the next pitch,
some dirty sleight-of-hand down and away
he'd picked up somewhere
in the Mexican League. Done,
he'd trudge in from the mound.
His tired, mangy face had no illusions.
But the first curve I ever threw
that worked astonished me
as much as the lefty clean-up man I faced.
He dropped, and when I grinned
smiled weakly back. What he'd seen
I couldn't even guess
until one tepid evening in the Pony League
I stepped in against a southpaw,
a kid with catfish lips
and greased-back hair,
who had to be too stupid
to know any magic tricks. He lunged,
smote one at my neck.
I ducked. Then, either
that ball's spin broke every law
I'd ever heard about or else
Morris County moved almost
a foot. I was out
by the cheapest trick the air

can pull—Bernoulli's Principle.
Like "magic," the common love songs
wail and are eager to repeat
it helplessly, *magic,* as if to say
what else can one say, it's *magic,*
which is the stupidest of words
because it stands for nothing:
there is no magic. And yet
what other word does the heartbroken
or the strikeout victim have
to mean what cannot be and mean what is.

Ulysses and the Sirens

I never had much curiosity
about that first queasy step
down on the moon. But who hasn't
hankered secretly to know exactly
what Ulysses heard or saw?
Who hasn't envied him a little
shackled to his mast when the swells
of their oiled thighs began
unrolling from the oily thighs
of the ocean's slow swells
and their pale limbs lifting
from the water's turning limbs
came turning toward him,
and they rose one after another
like knowledge from the water,
up from that green library, the sea,
flashes of their bare shoulders
climbing from the water's flashing
shoulders, their faces drenched,
still sightless in the passion
of the water. I'd like
to think that no matter how dizzying
their song, Ulysses' gaze—oh,
he was curious—picking the nearest
one, would have gone straight
to her pubic zone—
that where there should have been
a wedge of hair, exactly
there is where he zeroed in—
that while there was still time
before the sea, brandishing
its shields, its scales, its random

dents of light, covered her again,
he stared, as I, as any of us would,
not lewdly—scientifically—
failing, still, to apprehend exactly
where the first scale issued
from her skin, where either
of her ended or began.

Landscapes

near Moab, Utah

All morning, drifting among the tall
volumes of that rock library,
we kept our voices hushed as if those rocks—
great wrinkled scholars hunched against the sky—
were frowning over matters far
more momentous than we were,
while our voices, lightweight, silly
as the voices of schoolchildren
in such a company of elders, floated
about their shoulders, rolled off their backs.
Some landscapes invite us to fall in love
with them. Their features,
like the countenances of the very beautiful,
remain ambiguous, composite of so many
slowly dissolving human expressions
that, like the faces of the famous,
they promise intimacy with everyone
at once. Though they be eyeless,
though they hold their pose, perfectly demure,
it's as if the gaze of a shadow or a tree,
the empty gaze of even light itself
held some indication, could answer us.
Whichever way we turn, they turn
with us slightly. We stop. They stop,
waiting for us. Nothing moves.
Like beautiful women, the rocks return
our gaze, expectant. There is no need for speech.
Their gaze means everything at once.

Jealousy

Jealousy is no more a form of paranoia than is any other
art form that would locate some pattern in our experience.
—W. H. Finn

Without it nothing would make enough sense.
Alone, he listens for the grudging hush
of tires, her furtive dive home
as the family car swerves into their drive,
the neat, pat squeak of brakes,
a door slam—five minutes late.
A car sighs up the street, seems
to pause, passes, not his wife.
Already, the night teems with evidence.
How abstractly that morning
she'd milled her hair.
And the last time she got home this late—
how willing to explain it she had been.
The case, he nods grimly to himself,
is now almost complete.
No matter how much he hates what it says
he must follow up every lead.
Once again he goes over the scene—
a parked car perhaps, the streetlight's
sickly pallor on the hood,
how one last time she would hesitate,
then, with almost a sigh of relief,
give her mouth gradually to another man,
be whispering something urgent,
be kissing him again, unlocking slowly
an even deeper secret and unloosening it.
But it's not their silent grappling
on the seat, the minor clicks of passion,

it's not the bustle of clothing
which he wants. It's that hush
of the moment before, the threshold
when a gap in the conversation went
taut, redundant under the weight
of silence. That
is the moment on which he's come to count—
a moment when, each time he constructs it anew,
adds another harsh catch in his breath
and hurts him again, it hurts
even more, hurts so much
he no longer cares if it's true.

Shoptalk

I like this low, comfortable kind
of conversation which the rain's
been having with itself all day
as it goes about its business,
deftly assembling its tiny parts,
confident, in no great hurry,
discussing, perhaps, the different
gutters it has seen, the taste of rust
in New York, the rust in Chicago.
Or perhaps comparing notes
about the finer points of roofs,
where best to creep to find
flaws in asphalt shingles,
or maybe it's murmuring in rain-jargon
over different grades of redwood,
the rates they rot. No end of stories
that it could be telling—
the drudgery of cycling in a monsoon,
monotony of equatorial assignments,
the same steamy party each afternoon.
Or maybe the gossip's of some great
typhoon, the melee of another
grand convention. Or is it muttering
about the way some thunderstorms
rig their elections, the social
life of rain in some bayou,
as the rain keeps up its quiet
shoptalk—the level, reassuring
talk of people who are comfortable

again, sure what they're doing,
graceful in their work, and accurate,
serious in the way that rain
is serious, given over to their task
of touching the world.

Hotel Kitchen

We never saw the audience we served.
Downstairs in those steel kitchens, in the loud
Bucket brigade of orders, pots, and shuttling
of dishes hand-to-hand, you couldn't hear
the murmurous conversation of the rich
at lunch. But you could feel them, scented, laundered,
sitting on your head. You could feel it right
through the floor, feel it so well that when
we ran out of mashed potatoes once
and Cookie skimmed some off a garbage pail,
slapped it on a plate and dealt it off
to Hernandez, the Head Chef, who
flourished sauce on it and shipped it on,
our kitchen practically spluttered to a stop—
a glee we somehow managed
to strangle underground, tie up
the moment the manager strolled in.
I juggled the bakery's steel bowls and pans.
My buddy, Frank, tackled the garbage-can-size
stew pots, wept his sweat back in them
as he'd disappear headfirst, wrestling
them down to reach the bottom
and bark the black crust off.
Once you've served below the ground like that,
making the world materialize graciously above,
where hunger is a problem in chamber music—
once you've made chamber music in the kitchen,
if you love chamber music, you must love it
knowing what it means.

—for Jason

Sex without Love

If evil had style,
it might well resemble
those pointless experiments
we used to set up and run
with our legs and our hands
and our mouths between two
and four P.M. while our kids
were swimming in the public pool
and our wives, or husbands,
were somewhere else—
an hour when nobody wanted
to move, the heat
had gone breathless, slack
as if the afternoon
had been punched in the stomach,
a victim of what we'd coolly
decided to do. There might
be the nagging of a single mower.
At last even that would die
in the heat. We could catch
a rumor of thunder in the hills—
a signal, like the smirk
of swallowed amusement you'd slip
my direction by raising just
slightly your eyebrows as much
as to ask, *Well? Shall we?*
Its style might well resemble
the wholly gratuitous gear
we would then shift down to
as deliberately we would undress,
our eyes wide open, without
compromise, curious to observe what
a body might be up to next

on such a hopeless afternoon,
just barely affection
enough—a pinch of salt—
to produce that sigh, when
for a lucky moment or so
curiosity can be mistaken
for enthusiasm and we learn
what we already know.

for X

Against Paradise

Is there no change of death in paradise?
—Wallace Stevens

The hounds that heralded the rich
would wake us up at six
on Sunday morning, hounds begging
the very air for blood,
hounds poring over stones, zigzagging,
their avid noses thumbing
through the grasses, reading
our shabby field down by the swamp,
reading through our lawn,
an open library of appetites.
When, from cover in our rickety woods,
the fox hunters issued in a posse,
I'd pretend they were the British.
Outlaw in my pajamas, behind
the curtains, I'd draw my bead
on brokers, financiers, on girls
desexed in britches and strait coats,
on local names like Wheelwright, Miller,
Reeve, names with a quaint,
almost an ancient sound.

Miles from where they lived on higher ground,
like golfers or rare birds
errant in the rough,
they'd sit there, high
and in no hurry at all,
surveying our ramshackle little field
with its gnarled pear tree,
as if they were the owners
in their old costumes—redcoats
we could no longer recognize.

But later, when I'd mow the lawn,
not knowing any better,
I longed to give it the elegiac look
of their estates, thinned groves
arranged like furniture
within the neat ballroom of a field
where the grass, uniform and smooth
as indoor carpeting stretched wall-to-wall.

To show off your station (which is your name)
the grounds of your estate must be
conspicuously false and very trite—
the pond a polished table-top "like glass,"
the trees "stately," the pastures
"rolling" and "idyllic," the bases
of the bushes drained of leaves,
the farthest line of trees a hazy backdrop
for some diorama where, in the foreground,
kittens "sport" by a picnic basket,
fawns "gambol." Your dog,
like those dignified, melancholy dogs
varnished on the backs of playing cards,
should have a pedigree. It should maintain
a solemn, philosophical expression
and be named "Rex" or "Rusty."

Sometimes, Sunday afternoons, a rich kid
named Bradley Wheelwright asked me
over to his home to play.
The house was stifling.
It was crepuscular all day.
Always, Bradley's parents would be out,
the curtains drawn on parlors
muffled as stuffed birds, where Bradley
or the maid, like museum guards, cautioned
nothing must be touched,

as we trespassed over carpets thick
enough to suffocate our steps, past walls
of massive, leather novels, past stilled
encyclopedias, under chandeliers
and up a back staircase
to the upper stories, to the only
messy room in the whole place,
where, dutifully, Brad dragged
his Electric Baseball out.

And suddenly I'd wish that I were home
practicing my curve
against the south side of the garage,
my threadbare tennis ball alive
in the dead air—the only terms I had
back then for something I half knew but
hadn't yet learned how to say,
something about how monuments go bad,
how all that wealth can do
is to magnify a banal appetite,
but how it hangs on anyway, inherently,
like a species—this pure desire
that the names of things stay fixed
while customary services go on,
that the same torpid statuary
remain sprawled around the pool
up at the country club (a pool bluer
than the sky, a pool like glass),
nymph, fawn, satyr wired
in their casual positions,
secured in paradise—that all those precious, old,
well-tended, not-especially-happy names
might be made fast
high on some wall as if alive,
perfectly composed in their huge frames.

Oz

In Kansas the witches come in all colors;
they go in all directions when the wind weaves
the water dark over sloughs. They're slippery.
They easily get away, vanish into the pale
grasses. At night they ride the fields.
But in Oz there are only two witches.
You can spot the wicked one a mile away.
The single black object around, she's
a preposterous blot: black rags flapping
among the flowers, cursing the gay
Easter basket colors. For she's been exiled,
she's not allowed to associate with trees.
There is no shade there, nowhere to hide.
You could put your fist through the dyed
sugar landscape. The rocks chip if you
brush them too hard. Night doesn't come there
any more: it's an empty threat. The bats
circling drearily at noon are easily picked off.
The birds cheep cheerily year after year,
canned laughter. It will always be this way.
If the Wicked Witch's rags acquired the luster
of a raven's coat, a rainbow shine
in bituminous wings, just as she started
to grow transparent, a flash of wind across
the grasses, just as she was about to vanish,
before the spectrum was sewn in the waters,
a humming would come from the south,
the cheerful hum of her sister, the Good Witch,
Glinda, retouching the leaves with her wand.
One spray of her scented smile
would deaden the Wicked Witch while she
tidied the waters, straightened the flowers
and made the colors fast.

Tumbleweed

Arms with hands grasping seek to clutch at the prows.
Bodies thrown recklessly in the way are cut aside.
  —William Carlos Williams

This morning the March wind is huge, and there are many of them
struggling across the fields, but they travel singly.
They do not know each other. Sometimes one, like a chicken
just beheaded, shudders in a spasm across the road,
gets caught on a bumper, and the car wears it for awhile
like a badge, though it stands for nothing, a poor man's jewelry,
a burr. A fat one, like the architecture
of a small cumulus cloud, hesitates in the right-hand lane,
makes its move. "Hit it!" my son urges. Wind buffets us.
We catch it flush, feel its shriveled limbs clutch
the bumper and, clinging, travel with us, its weightless anatomy
continuing in a new direction, perpendicular
to the rest of their southern migration
as we forge westward through it, casting guilty glances
north where more of them are bouncing in the distance, bouncing
in place, and we notice, closer, the barbed wire hedge,
how they are plastered to it, stuck, clawing like insects
begging, determined to climb it and to cross
the highway. *Why did the chicken cross the road?* Tourists,
we stare out the window at fields, a roaring tundra
spread-eagled under the force of the sky, at the tumbleweed
endlessly bobbing toward us as if eager for something,
and feel a kind of pity for the dead, who are truly homeless,
at the way the body, when it's shed its soul
is physically driven on, regardless, a bristle of matter. Wind
leans on the car, and we wonder if we, ourselves, aren't

being buffeted across some frigid field as randomly
as these mops of tumbleweed snagged on the barbed-wire
perimeter, shivering there in a row, miles of prisoners
facing the moat they have to get across
as the gods sail by all day, at sixty miles an hour, free.

The Wisdom Tooth

In the days when it was still stupendous
to be a "millionaire," I thought money
was something you could fan
out all over the floor, like what we toted home
on Halloween, in shopping bags,
the salary that all us children got
for doing the only job we knew how to do—
going to school, addressing grownups in falsetto
solemnly, being cute. But when at last
alone, skipping the peanuts, the endless
jelly beans (useless as pennies),
skipping Mrs. Garrity's homemade cookies,
skipping even Ackermans' fresh apples,
we delved straight to the bottom of the bag,
scrounging for the jackpot, a candy bar.
Glittering in its star-spangled wrapper
like some early Christmas present from Las Vegas,
a Milky Way gave off a tiny halo; it seemed
to float above the floor, a minor
miracle. We craved only the most tawdry stuff,
junk so sweet its sugars
almost hurt your head to eat—
the very thing, my fourth-grade teacher, Mrs. Lee,
with a vinegar expression on her mouth,
promised us could rot the character
of Eagle Scouts, of even the whitest,
four-square Christian teeth.
The world beyond that window
(she made this clear) is booby-trapped.
There were little pills, she hissed,
that made a boy feel powerful, so good
that if you popped just one into your mouth
you wanted more and more: you couldn't stop.

And so, each week she trotted out
this trusty wisdom tooth she kept
in a glass of stale Pepsi, and we would peer
into the amber glass museum
where that lucky tooth basked in its corruption—
a tooth gone soft, its edges slurred with rust,
"Probably in pain," said Mrs. Lee.
And we would nod solemnly
and play along with her, dreaming
of someday being millionaires, of buying
all the Milky Ways and all the Mars Bars
and nougat-dripping, thick Forever Yours
we'd ever wanted, and dream
of the forbidden and delicious world,
about which Mrs. Lee would drop her voice
and speak in confidence to us,
of being corrupt.

Some Basic Aesthetics

Out past the motels where town ends
and all the weather starts and the windy
grasses are rattling their dried bracelets,
Greg swung his pickup off the dusty road,
and we wobbled westward over ruts, looking
for some place safe to shoot.
What does being "American" feel like?
Steering the sights of his .357 magnum
from lucky rock to rock, I could feel
the solid handshake of its grip adjusting
me again in the comfortable old stance
that cap pistols set us in as boys.
Our trigger fingers light, whimsical,
we'd point, peremptory, directing
that hypothesis from tree to rock to darting
Indian to Kraut. This stance redoubled us
as in the batter's box, bats cocked.
Drop your guns. Keep your hands up. I expected
someday to own guns, to wear a tie.
Steering the magnum's trustworthy weight, sparing
a bush, sparing a dry patch, sparing a tree,
I parked my sights in front of a rock
where, on flatter ground, third base might be.
If it's possible to "feel" American,
it was the first *Bam* boxing both my ears, numbing
half my face as, *Bam,* the limestone flared
a whiff of smoke, went out. *Bam.*
The valley harvested another crop of echoes
broadening into luxurious redundancy
upon redundancy. It was the thrill
of having your hands on so many cylinders
at once, all of them extra,
more capability than I would ever need.

Full Circle

for Alan Nordby Holden (1904–1985)

Scared, I watch my son, eleven, his first
time on the mound, stare in
at the tiny lead-off man.
So tense he's poker-faced,
Zack's practicing the politician's trick
of looking confident, as if a man
could be substantial just by looking it.
But pitching, I learned young, isn't politics.
In the center of that dusty ring
where, as if under some unremitting examination
by the lights, your squirmy shadow's multiplied
by five, faking doesn't work.
The one thing not to do, I told him earlier,
is issue walks. We were playing catch.
I whipped one back. I was talking
as casually as I could, worried
about tonight, but trying to hide it,
to talk seductively. I was talking
in teasy little parables, embroidering them—
about the time I walked eight batters in a row,
about the time I got mad at the umpire
and started to cry—anything to make sure
what help I gave the boy would register
before he'd be alone there on the mound,
out of range. His low fastball stung
my hand. I whipped it back. I told him
how sometimes in the middle of a game
if you get wild you can think about
your stride or where your shoulders face,
you can experiment, correct yourself.
As I talked and threw and talked, we never broke
the easy to-and-fro of pitch and catch,

the more I talked the better
I remembered how. I understood
my own shock when my father used to pause
from his obsessive work to talk to me, to offer—
always shrewdly, at a slight oblique—
what help he could. Zack throws.
The batter takes. Ball one. Ball two. Ball three.
And I prepare myself for the first of many walks.
Zack pauses, on the next pitch eases up.
It's nicked foul. Impassive, Zack waits
for the ball. He delivers easy,
call strike two. If the advice is right
and handed out with style,
we never forget the things our fathers say.
They talk directly to our sons,
and our sons can deliver us
our own boyhood back a second time.
The batter whiffs. We live redundantly,
and the second time is better than the first.

from

american gothic

1992

Atlantis

We cannot guess the true girth of an oak
until one has capsized,
when the full spread of its root-attachment,
like a lost continent
submerged a lifetime in the earth
surfaces, a massive hull rolled
into the light,

and on the fulcrum of the oak's thousand elbows
it teeters,
an earthen island, like a man's heart
exposed, for the first time ever
beached in the plain air, drying
like the parts of a man who
for a moment has peeled away from his lover
and reclines topsy-turvy, blinking
at the world upside down at the world,
feet off the ground.

An oak may sprawl like this all morning,
scarcely stirring, remembering
the blackish-green exotic shades of the tornado,
how when fear is so articulated
it becomes beauty.
And, though for now the oak lies exhausted,
if an oak were conscious of itself, it would dream

of being righted again, its heart returned
to its body where the heart belongs
in the earth itself, remembering
how the burden of its root-system
had fit its excavation in the first world,

before that concavity, and dreaming,
if an oak dreams, words
to the earth:

I am your tree.

The Colors of Passion

The colors of passion are often mistakenly thought to be
shades of red; however its true colors are black and green.
—Sigmund Freud

The northwest starts hatching something so black
against it the landscape arches
dry, quarried out of chalk.
A squall-line raises the curtains
on this gymnasium of sky.
I forget my dignity.
I live underground with the deer mice, listening,
all ears, listening, remembering
the real thing.
She called me to the west window.
The sky was a war advancing toward us
ushering a freakish cloud,
a cobra, swaying,
tumescent, the sky's gray tongue.
People picked up by extra-terrestrials testify
how paralyzed they got, quivering
in the magnetic field of such pure panic
they were like the laboratory mice
we used to watch in the Bronx-Zoo snake house,
quivering under the judicial scrutiny
of a rattlesnake, they could
they could   hardly move   they let
its lightning tongue explore them. The sky kept coming,
these ugly remnants writhing in formation;
it was Biblical, the most intentional
sky I ever hope to see,
the sky armed with a gray sword.
The sword slid back into those low sheathes.

The sky charged us; it rode
over the roof and onward, east.
And around our shaky perch the curtains
closed, leaving us shuddering
in the shelter of each other
as if once more the world had spared us,
had left us only wet and harmless
as the birds outside
accepting the rain like the grass,
and the grass flagrant and greener,
more serious than ever.

Cancer

Insidious. fr. L. *insidiae* an ambush, *fr. in* +
sedere to sit

> Sarcoma. Melanoma. Carcinoma. -*Oma.*
> If hatred is a form of worship
> I worship the -*Omas,*
> this family of tutelary deities.
> They're like the mockingbird.
> (People who are doomed look just like us.)
> When Richard Hugo had his lung removed,
> I wasn't surprised.
> I remembered 1979 (when he was alive),
> how, like a fat baby giving suck,
> he'd alternate mechanically between two tits—
> whisky, unfiltered cigarettes. Back and
> forth. Whisky. Cigarettes. It looked as if
> he'd set out some time ago, almost scientifically
> to kill himself. But there was a joker
> in his deck. When three years later for the last time
> we spoke over the telephone,
> the weathered saddle of his voice
> filtered through the atmosphere of long distance
> was wearing thin—the voice, pausing
> to fetch breath,
> listless, and faint   and faint   almost
> out of reach   sighed,
> "It's not the smoking kind."
> It was *leukemia.*
>
> During her last ten years, my mother
> suffered fitfully from lower back pains
> diagnosed as *osteoporosis.*

It was a trick. Multiple myeloma likes
to wear costumes: it likes to mimic
other little gods. -*Oma*. Actual death is usually
"indirect," of a secondary cause,
often pneumonia. Your ribs, riddled
with it, get rickety, frail
as sticks of chalk, begin to crack until
like the rotten pilings in a mine
they give; the shaft fills up.
She was closing a window
when, much to her surprise, her hand—
her lovely hand, fragile
as a bouquet of shriveled stalks—
just simply broke.
Her bones were caving in
like a house-frame eaten out by termites
from the inside. Test with your pen-knife
the wrong stud and your blade
bursts through this paper-thin veneer
you could have sworn was wood
into a brown cavity, into the ruins of a city
like Dresden. The stud is fraudulent.
The house is fraudulent.
The last time I saw her (when she was alive)
she was lying stricken like a shot doe
on her back, in traction. She was confused.
Only her eyes were independent.
Her body, so like the person I had loved,
was hardly hers: it was
a facsimile.

I had believed
that with my family's history of health
I was immune. I hear the mockingbird.
It *is* my family. -*Oma*.

But where is it nested?
What angle is it coming from?
Is it the bird? Is it the mask?
It's a dirty trick. It's
everywhere, it's insidious it squirts
around so fast. It's like a thief, a myth,
smoke-in-the-air! It looks like you and me.
It smiles and shakes your hand as if
you'd asked it home for dinner.
Is this the mask? You can't be sure.
-*Oma!* I just thought I heard it. Far
far off. It was singing again, O,
like a nightingale.

The Crash

October, 1987, Wall Street

i. Tuesday, 10/6/87

Passion was supposed to be great fun,
like a roller-coaster ride, scary,
but you never risk your life, he thinks.
No one talks about the other side
of being "in love," the work it is,
the obligations of adultery,
like holding down a second full-time job.
Moonlighting, he thinks, as he shaves, pleased
with the turn this turn of phrase has taken.
All summer, Tuesdays and Thursdays, as if
to attend some special seminar
on schedule at noon sharp, he emerges
from the tinted-glass mirroring panoply
of the brokerage. The Fifth Avenue bus
comes swinging in, brakes sneezing; he swings
aboard. Clenched secretly inside
like a man straddling a knife-blade,
he's borne uptown to her basement apartment.
He'll lock the door, turn to her.
They'll welcome each other with a hug,
and now a kiss (the kind that opens
gradually like a fissure,
swallows us.) And so, without more fuss,
they'll strip and efficiently every-
which-way slip into each other.

"Habit of production," Aristotle
called art, "according to right method."

Six months of doing it, and they
can ply their trade
deftly as a pair of licensed plumbers,
or like two potters, both professionals,
wedging and centering the clay
without a fuss. They can do it
with maximum tenderness. Can do it
with sudden, passionate squalls, with sobs
or laughter. With whispers. This
is serious play. Adult play. Adultery.
After much practice, they begin
to call their different lunch-hours "poems."
They rate them afterward.
"That was one of our best poems," he murmurs
two hours later on the phone. "Yes,"
she breathes. Then silence
as they think about their "poem,"
though he's not a poet. He has contempt
for poetry, he only likes the *word* (her word).

He likes the idea of what he thinks
it is. Something about flowers. Birds.
And bees. A kind of pink decorum. For him
the real poetry is money,
and in a way he's right. Money *is*
a kind of poetry. But he wouldn't call it that.
What Coleridge called "that willing
suspension of disbelief that is poetic faith"
he'd call "leverage," he'd call it "credit."
"Yes," she sighs, "it was a lovely poem.
It left me sleepy." She sighs again.
It's October 6. It's 2:30 in the afternoon.
The poetry of money is being read out.
The Dow Jones Industrial is hovering at 2640,

a new high. The prime lending rate is 8.75.
His attention wanders from the ticker tape.
His every surface is so freshly painted
he can sense its glistening. It's not dry yet.
He's coated with her sex, his hands
so sticky with it that, surreptitiously,
he touches his fingers to his lips, tastes
his own skin to catch a whiff of her.
It's siesta time. Sitting upright,
he seems to doze awake.
The bond market is steady at this hour.
AT&T is flirting with an all-time high
near 37. He'd like a jelly doughnut.
He wonders what his wife will cook for supper.

ii. 10/19/87, Black Monday

Noon. The bus comes swinging in, doors
wheeze open. He enters blindly. The weather's
pretty, yet (He can't quite put
his finger on it) false.
Ever since that Wednesday, October 7,
when the Fed jacked up the prime
a full half point, sending the Dow stumbling
90 points downstairs
to close at 2516,
the market's been subject to odd moods.
Down 34 that Friday, even further down
last Friday—down 57 points—
and it's headed down today. He needs
something to relax him.
She strips efficiently; he fumbles at his belt.
He checks his watch. She notices
how compulsively he checks his watch.
He doesn't take it off. No one could possibly

know his whereabouts right now, yet he acts
as if at any second the telephone is going to ring
for him. "Are you okay?" she asks. "Sure."
She draws the curtains closed.
But, flopped on the waterbed, one arm flung
limply over her flank, he finds himself unable
to make the usual "poem." He's imagining
instead his office telephone ringing
three-quarters of a mile away and ringing.
And ringing. Money, like a screaming
infant, requiring attention immediately, *this
instant,* while he lies here, helpless, pitying
his poor, distracted penis. It's like the market.
Neither will go up.

Outside the midday sun shines uninterrupted
in a major key. The sky is blue, without a blemish.
The real world seems not the least aware
of this other weather, an exotic weather only he
can see, The Market—told only in the barometer.
That she is real—her tongue and teeth real
as raw oysters on the half-shell—
should reassure him. And that she is here
while billions of dollars are ceasing to exist.
They're not going up in smoke or steam. They're
not going anywhere. There is no "where" for money.
No "here." Or "there." *Honey,
are you okay?* He cannot answer her.
Because he's neither here nor there.

from

the sublime
1996

Gould

> I say: a flower! and out of the oblivion into which
> my voice consigns every outline, apart from the known
> calyxes, there arises musically, the delicate idea itself,
> the flower absent from all bouquets.
>   —Stephane Mallarme

i.

There are two ways of doing everything:
talking, making music, making love.
One is human. To err is human. The violinist
sweats. Maybe, like Glenn Gould on the keyboard
he sings along. Gould hummed so loud
he can be heard
on the master tapes. Maybe he groans.
The violin requires
strength. One's shoulder starts to hurt,
cramp up. I remember, in the middle
of a weekday morning making love
a cramp blinking on, a light-bulb
burning in my right calf
like a screaming newborn
exacting my attention.
No choice except to climb out of bed
and stand on my right leg
and bear down
to try to placate it,
then go back to bed,
recover the warm lining
of the dream that we'd been in,
breathing closely

on the coals, hoping
they will blush and blink
back to life,
that before 1 P.M.,
when we would have to
pull our clothes back on and drive to work,
we could create a condition
so like music we would be able
to take it with us secretly
like a melody, say the opening
of Bach's *Die Kunst Der Fugue*
right at the knot which the viola
like a caught breath, almost a sob,
ties as it begins to overlap
the second violin
which, though praising God,
has become the tide, seems
already to be grieving steadily.

ii.

Glenn Gould last publicly performed
on April 10, 1964. He wrote,
The presence of the audience
is impossible to reconcile
with the essentially private act
of music-making,
that music was best served
by the recording studio,
by any medium which permits one
the luxury of second-guessing
the interpretive decision.
From then on, like the Princess and the pea,
unable to play when the piano bench
might be a sixteenth of an inch

too high,
he thought as Stephane Mallarme, who wrote,
In the pure work the poet
disappears, yields his place to the words
taking light from mutual reflection—
like an actual train of fire over precious stones
replacing the human direction
of the phrase.
It is not from basic sonorities
made by brass and strings and woodwind
that music will emerge in clarity.

iii.

I'm not sure when it was
I began to understand
the world's orders to us are inherently
contradictory: that to be adult
well is to live naively, to live
as though you didn't know you're going to die,
make love to cramped ecstatic paradox.
Johann Sebastian Bach,
whose music Gould liked best, Gould,
the purist, could still praise as
valuable for its humanity.
All that time, until he died at fifty,
he'd been singing along,
human in spite of himself.
I remember singing Bach, in choirs.
Hearing the other parts was like standing
within the structure of a thunderhead,
glimpsing from the corner of an eye
flesh-tones of sunlight catching
on a furling cornice
while the graying roofs below

keep tumbling, and you're being
buoyed by this updraft
out of yourself, drawing
breath to sing, human, helpless, knowing,
hardly knowing what you're doing.

Knowing

i.

My son, at eight, would want to save the life
of the plate-eyed deer mouse
the cat occasionally carried home
to tutor for an afternoon.
She'd drop it on the rug, and sock it in the head
till it felt sick and wanted to go home
and wobbled up to the teacher to ask, "Please?
I don't feel well. May I go home?"
but the teacher smiled, "Stop being a sissy,"
and swiped it in the head
until the new pupil was bewildered,
felt sicker in the stomach,
and would've cried except it was too scared,
and the teacher was talking: "Run!" "Stop!"
"Sit down!" "Raise your hand!"
"Shit in your pants!" "Run!"
"Sit down!" "Limp!" "That's it!"
"Break a leg!" "Run!" "That's it!"
"Break your neck!" "Run!"
"Throw up!" "That's it!" She would
encourage it, ration out its hope
till it could be stored
beneath the sofa like a toy
and be counted on to cooperate.
In half an hour it would be released
like a little old man from the hospital.
Gamely, totteringly, he'll venture from cover
out into the light, offer himself again,
hoping that school is over.

ii.

Go! The children lined along the sidelines
are shrieking in a way they'd never
shriek over arithmetic
as the differences between fast and slow
widen and grow until it's glaring
as a scream, a public obscenity—All men are *not* created equal—
the truth we must pretend we cannot see,
don't even know about, even
as it's being repeated louder until
the winners burst lightly through the tape
and are already banking gracefully away
to accept their ribbons
as if they'd known the outcome in advance.

iii.

The man and the woman love
to talk when they're making love,
though not all the time.
Sometimes they'll let themselves die
by drowning. Sometimes
they'll watch themselves drown. They don't need
any equipment. No mirrors. Only some words.
A code. Protection from spies.
Mmm! Sweetcorn! Equipment,
they laugh, is for the birds,
for the bourgeoisie.
The rest don't know.
They take things—an arm, a shoulder—
literally. Sometimes, during their deaths
and rebirths, the man and the woman
like to watch themselves
as they do it. *As if our bodies*

were a couple of puppies,
she sighs. They marvel:
how the more they do it the more
deeply they love each other.
Then they laugh about how naive
was the boys' belief
that "strange" is attractive, about how
the more deeply they come
to understand the art
of familiarity, the faster
it snowballs, the more they know
the more they want more love.
And the more they know, the more
they know what they know
what they know
of love.

The Third Party

Her mind
was so much more than she—
it was a third party.
Like some large instrument
at the love-bed,
it made an exotic guest: able
to decide on its own
whether or not to participate.

Hurt people bear with them
a slightly puzzled look,
a scar between the eyes
where their grief is lodged,
a lead plummet.
I'd seen her, a scientist, delve
into a differential
equation like a boy rudely
unlocking an orange by
forcing the seams from the lobes
to spring it open.
But as she analyzed her rotten marriage,
she was plain stupid.

There is no one, I think,
whose private life isn't more
or less unlovely than daily weather.
It's the country where our friends
all speak the same tongue.
Whatever you do,
every angle of the bones,
has been tried before,
and the speech of grief,

a dead end in itself,
so satisfying, so useless,
is the same tautology, the last
cliché, the one area of expertise
in which, sooner or later,
we get as good as anybody.

As she talked, her hand on mine,
heavy, opaque, and sad,
her heartbeat a mute syllable
typed out in code,
her beautiful mind—so
much better than she—could no more
save her than the pure
scaffolding of chamber music
as it goes up
can save the four, short
scholarly men huddled under it,
a quartet of carpenters
with too much on their hands,
measuring, filing, conferring
like mad to assemble
another section of an intelligence
almost too plausible.

Like a calculated smile, it,
too, might break
a man's heart or save
his life,
but is, indeed, heartless,
better than we are,
hardly any help at all.

Love in the Time of Cholera

Those of us who have grown addicted
to long, long-distance sighs,
static-filled gaps over a telephone
can still remember
the re-enactable, lingering potency
of the old-fashioned *billet doux.*
They understand fully the difference
between "Dear _____" and "Dearest."
Tearing a letter open, they have experienced
the vertiginous chasm between
the polite, equivocal "Yours"
and the naked "Your,"
the vulgarity of "Darling." They know
how in *Amor en El Tiempo del Colera*
Ferdinando wins Fermina with letters,
how single-mindedly, like Don Quixote,
he invents his own romance—
that *Amor,* at its truest, like a book,
sets its words down tremblingly
faithfully in cursive,
that it is when one is struggling
like a bee fallen in the bathtub
to keep afloat, stay eye-level
with the surface, in order
to see where he is
that a man will resort to the clichés
I love you, I adore you—
desperate shorthand for matters
too incendiary to be touched
except by an adequate music,
by a poetry capable of breathing
life into the gray coal

of even the lowliest syllable.
Laboring, up late, alone
on a letter answering a letter,
retracing tenderly as if
by fingertip its tentative words,
retracing a word and retracing it,
at times, they are startled by a bee-sting.
Though in pain themselves, instead
of groaning, they chuckle privately, pitying
those poor souls who may never
possess the world enough,
for whom love ended with the telephone.

Gulf: January 17, 1991

Ah, love, let us be true
To one another!
   —Matthew Arnold

And didn't our love seem almost a political act,
to turn away from the footage of the F-15s
following each other in single file
along a slow assembly line as if on parade,
toy after toy, each copy being lifted, smoking
off the scorched belt, then the next
and the next being mass-produced into an industrial sky.
As we kissed, and kissed more deeply, trying
to make the picture go away, to deny this, I saw
that what we had been watching, what so fascinated us
was only another kind of factory, that it was inevitable
the activity we call "war" be conducted in round-the-clock shifts,
that military bases and state penitentiaries
are designed to manufacture identical deaths
as heartlessly as a commercial egg factory
where the lights are kept on to get the hens
to produce eggs faster than is natural. The men
all in the same sand-and-spinach uniform
were as similar as hens. Even the general strutting
like a fat rooster had donned those funny pajamas
like a surgeon's gown, a carpenter's apron—
what boys wear when they put on
the frightening costumes of efficiency,
roll up their sleeves and get ready to get down
to business, to be men. Wasn't it Spengler
who said it takes about twenty years for hens to forget,
for a generation to be bred ignorant of the shop floor,
enough time for new men who,

because they don't know any better, are willing
to put on the killing pajamas, the aprons again
and, like their grandfathers, earnestly go to work?
Isn't it twenty years since I used to watch, rapt,
with field glasses, the fleas circling
the hive of Alameda Naval Air Station,
the carrier like a slate, shelved landform
that would appear overnight, a gray grandmother,
to babysit the skyline for a week,
then go back to work in Asia. Ah, Love,
didn't it seem subversive to turn off the TV,
how we followed each other wordless, deep
into the immediate truth of the next kiss.
And the next. And decided then and there
we would take our costumes off for the afternoon,
we would not go to work that day
or the next. Or the next.

—for Ana

Karate

Mel Brown was teaching us
logic: First soften your opponent.
Seize the hair like a housewife
snapping lint from a rug and
snap. Or break one arm, blind him
with the splinters of his own
nose and so make him available
for the greater mechanical advantage
of both your elbows,
the next link in an argument
leading straight to the mat.
Mel checked us again.
A welterweight, he was forged
like a wedge, perfect.
On the glistening basalt of his chest
your fist could break.
Daintily
as some finicky high-
fashion photographer coaxing
a girl's surly chin,
cajoling, tilting her head by
fingertip to hold a pose,
he retouched our stances, adjusted
my knee, my drooping
elbows, the tickling flatteries
of his attentions pleasant
as the fussings of a barber.
Satisfied, he stepped
back. He was, as that saying goes,
undressing us with his eyes
he was snapping
our pictures.

Integrals

Erect, arched in disdain,
the integrals drift from left
across white windless pages
to the right,
serene as swans.
Tall,
beautiful seen from afar
on the wavering water, each
curves with the balanced severity
of a fine tool weighed in the palm.

Gaining energy now, they
break into a canter—stallions
bobbing the great crests of their manes.
No one suspects their power
who has not seen them rampage.
Like bulldozers, they build
by adding
dirt to dirt to stumps added
to boulders to broken glass added
to live trees by the roots added
to hillsides, to whole
housing developments
that roll, foaming before them,
the tumbling end of a broken wave
in one mangled sum: dandelions, old
beer-cans and broken
windows—gravestones all
rolled into one.

Yes, with the use of tables
integration is as easy as that:
the mere squeeze of a trigger, no
second thought. The swans
cannot feel the pain
it happens so fast.

Faking

Watching my daughter inclining
to her flute in grade-school band,
I remember straining to keep
my handhold in that creaking,
wheezing junkyard of bad sound
until I'd fallen behind;
I could hear the band going
on parting like water
in a brook around
a rock—me—and closing
loudly beyond while I waited
left behind, listening
in a kind of vertigo
(*What if I get caught?*)
almost as lonely as the time
years later, I found myself
on the cliff's face, slinging
a hammer to set pitons, listening
to the rock: *tink, tink, tink?*
attending to how each blow should register
a half-tone higher,
my very being attuned
to three true tones, questioning
the rock. A three-word question:
Three: blind: mice?
Then ascending a half-
step to set the next one
and listening, relying
on music, calling it

to account, being
called—*Three: blind: mice?*
to account, vowing
once again, never
to lie again.

The Sublime

Tell me, Jim, have you read Heidegger?
You're a professional weatherman.
That means we're both phenomenologists
like him. We study and forecast things
that we perceive. I once dismissed him
as a crank. I found it ludicrous
the big question he would ask
and ask again: *Wherein*
is the ground of Being,
until one day, six months ago,
on this breezy April afternoon
I encountered a weather that I'd heard
about but hadn't ever seen first hand.
A kind of front (a secret one) encroached
from the northwest—a front
of nothingness
all along my left side.

My first thought was "tumor,"
but a CAT scan saw nothing. I submitted
to an MRI. And there it was.
On an illuminated screen, the neurologist
fit a dozen black and white transparencies.
How like the contact sheets they were
from snapshots of the earth, filmed
from our nightly weather satellite.
There were the outlines of both hemispheres.
Those white spots, he explained,
which look like the radar blips of thunderstorms
were lesions.
It was the classic profile of MS.
Except for the numbness,

I did not feel ill.
Yet I *was* ill,
theoretically.

Jim, I used to think that "The Sublime"
was what Wordsworth meant
when he said he'd been "fostered alike
by beauty and by fear."
He talked about Nature as his mother:
"Her." He glimpsed Her in the landscape.
She frightened him.
Or it was the kind of pleasant vertigo
an English lord might feel
as a spectator at the park overlook
beholding the Matterhorn
or studying from a museum bench
a painting of the Matterhorn.
I remember rafting on the Arkansas
outside of Salida. Sometimes, as the raft
dove off a rock shelf and I was staring up
at a mountain range about
to crash on me, I knew
I was about to die
and yet I wasn't
really going to,
and knew
that later I would recollect it
with a delicious shudder.

This was different.
As I studied the pictures
of the landscape taken from orbit
after orbit over my own inner weather,
I marveled at the time-lapse
between the forecast on the screen

and my fate. If there were any horror,
it was at how *little* emotion I could feel.
This was knowledge I had no use for.
I remembered a friend who,
though at risk for AIDS, decided
quite rationally to forego
having his blood tested for HIV,
reasoning that if he tested positive
he would not want to know.
My fate was equally
theoretical.
This is the modern Sublime, Jim.
It is fear
made theoretical.
It's as if you were a spectator
to some one else's personal disaster
on TV.

Jim, though I'm a weatherman,
and, of course, I *do* know better
scientifically,
it seems I'm still inclined
like a romantic
the read the weather in my mood.
I remember when a cold front would come through,
magnificent and final, the night sky
jibbering with light, constantly
jumping and answering, signaling
madly to itself like Lear.
I know it's sentimental.
But now, simply remembering
that way to be afraid
when I was a child,
when I thought that one could hide

inside the covers
is comforting,
as if there were a place anywhere
inside or outside
to hide from this, some place.

Western Meadowlark

Through the open car window
seven needles in a haystack
BoPEEP-doodle-our-PEOple!
snatched by ear out of the moving
prairie, like you
already fading, passed, gone.
BoPEEP-doodle-our-PEOple!
If I could find it, it would be
points of sunlight glancing
off a brooch so near shades
of gold in these moving
grasses I could scarcely distinguish
it from the grasses. Like you
it is always gone.

BoPEEP-doodle-our-PEOple!
The bird pulled it off like a string
of catches on this flying
trapeze which keeps swinging
back. If birds' songs simply mean
I'm here! I'm here!
then why a song so baroque?
How many notes did it have?
Which notes were extra?

In the Beatles' "Blackbird"
you can hear a meadowlark, its song
canned as the slow-motion replay
of a pass-reception on TV:
Love studied into pornography,
Bo-PEEP-diddle-diddle-her-PEEP-hole!
The bird falls off a see-saw,

hesitates, picks itself
back up on the rising board,
completes its song.
It does it again.

I prefer the song that eludes me,
this one which we are passing,
banjo music picked out
through wind and distance
already falling behind

gone and not gone.

—for Ana